THE CIVIL WAR
ITS
PHOTOGRAPHIC HISTORY

THE WAR IN THE EAST

MATHEW B. BRADY AT BULL RUN, 1861

THE CIVIL WAR

ITS

PHOTOGRAPHIC HISTORY

THE WAR IN THE EAST

Compiled from actual photographs taken at the time of action by

MATHEW B. BRADY AND OTHERS

Edited by

JOSEPH B. EGAN, L.L.D.

and

ARTHUR W. DESMOND
Brigadier General of the Line
National Guard of the United States

Processing of Plates and Studio Work
JOHN D. PAYNE

CHARACTER BUILDING PUBLICATIONS
Wellesley Hills, Mass.

THE VISUAL HISTORY SERIES
THE CIVIL WAR

Printed in The United States of America

PREFACE

In 1839, twenty-two years before the Civil War began, the first practical "sun pictures" were made by a Frenchman named Daguerre. The story goes that Mathew Brady, to whom we are indebted for most of the beautiful pictures in this series, having gone to Europe with the inventor of the electric telegraph, Samuel F. B. Morse, met Daguerre and was so impressed by what he learned that he determined to devote his life to the photographic art. Brady was at that time a boy of sixteen.

We know that, early in the forties, Mathew Brady opened the first sky-lighted photographic studio in New York and that he was responsible to a marked degree for the perfection of the daguerreotype process. In the years that followed, young Brady became the most popular photographer in America, as the following quotation from Bret Harte would indicate.

> *Well, yes—if you saw us out driving*
> *Each day in the Park, four-in-hand—*
> *If you saw poor dear mamma contriving*
> *To look supernaturally grand,—*
> *If you saw papa's picture, as taken*
> *By Brady, and tinted at that,—*
> *You'd never suspect he sold bacon*
> *And flour at Poverty Flat.*

Mathew Brady has the unique distinction of having photographed every President of the United States from John Quincy Adams to William McKinley, with the one exception of Benjamin Harrison, who died before the picture could be taken.

When hostilities began between the North and the South, Brady went at once to Washington to get permission to go into the field with the army in order to make a photographic record of the war in the interests of historical truth. With him went Alexander Gardner, the English "wet-plate" expert and a large corps of assistants. Brady financed the entire cost of this patriotic effort from the fortune he had made in New York.

Lack of appreciation was the fate of Mathew Brady, as it has been the fate of so many other great men of genius. After spending four precious years and one hundred thousand dollars in the great work of preserving the photographic history of the Civil War, Brady died neglected, alone, and without funds, in a New York Hospital. With eyesight failing, and a body crippled by an accident, his last years were bitter in the extreme.

Brady's failure to profit by his work was partly due, of course, to the fact that there was no way of reproducing his beautiful pictures in book form. The present method of transferring them to copper or zinc by photo-engraving, did not come into common use until about the time of his death, in 1896.

The editors, hopeful that their work may be, in a sense, a memorial to Mathew B. Brady and his co-workers have drawn on all available sources of photographic materials.

As a means of presenting the history of the Civil War, these pictures are unique. They *breathe* history,—every one of them,—the history of a brave day that has gone and of brave men, on both sides, who did not hesitate to lay down their lives for their convictions.

It is in this spirit that this edition of these photographs is offered to the public. Here is a contribution to an appreciation of the greatness of our country that the schools and homes can ill afford to lose. As these pictures are studied, the history of the great war between brothers will become clear, and the various battles and campaigns will emerge as thrilling episodes in the life of a people who have, in the short space of a few hundred years, conquered a wilderness and built upon it one of the world's greatest civilizations,—a civilization in which the principles of democracy and freedom have flowered and are flowering into a magnificent portrayal of man's hope of universal brotherhood.

The editors have tried to reduce the action in every engagement to its simplest terms. Even the names of most of the competing Generals have been eliminated. No attempt has been made to follow the confusing details of any battle. The charges and countercharges, both physical and political, have been left to the historian. Today, *all Americans are brothers* and the genius and heroism of "Stonewall" Jackson are as true examples of unfolding America, as the persistency and dogged determination of General Grant.

In looking at these pictures of a day that is long past, the beholder should keep in mind the following considerations: The "wet" plate of that distant day, from which each picture is derived, was very hard to preserve. Many of these glass plates, at this moment, are yellow and difficult to reproduce. Others have been cracked beyond repair, necessitating very delicate studio preparation before any printing can be done. Some of the pictures that seem dim were taken with the smoke of battle clouding the field, or with fog or drizzling rain whirling before the lens of the camera. More than all else, one must remember that each picture is a *time exposure*. There were no snapshots in Mathew Brady's day. It was the artist's duty to sensitize his own plate, rush out and expose it, rush back to his field wagon where he had rigged up a darkroom and develop it, and then personally stand by on guard until it had had time to dry. The entire operation, exclusive of drying, could not consume more than eight minutes.

When these factors are considered, the remarkable fact remains that, here are actual views taken from these old sources that, for sheer beauty of composition, artistry and stereoscopic depth, challenge the skill of the most favored modern photographer. As an instance of what is meant attention is directed to "Antietam Bridge", page 68.

Finally: This book, in its present beautiful form, would not have been possible without the aid of a new and unique discovery in the photographic field which has enabled the editors to capture and record for all time the original loveliness of these Brady pictures.

CONTENTS

MATHEW B. BRADY'S FIELD DARKROOM
Called by the soldiers of both sides the "What Is It" wagon

NORTHERN LEADERS

ULYSSES S. GRANT

WILLIAM TECUMSEH SHERMAN

SOUTHERN LEADERS

"STONEWALL" JACKSON

ROBERT E. LEE

THE FOUR GREAT GENERALS OF THE CIVIL WAR

THE FEDERAL CAPITOL
WASHINGTON IN 1863

THE CONFEDERATE CAPITOL
RICHMOND IN 1865

CHAPTER ONE

THE BATTLE OF BULL RUN

On the 12th of April, 1861, the Confederate forces fired the historic shots at Fort Sumter that began one of the bloodiest and most savagely fought wars in all history. It was not, however, until the 21st of July, in the same year, that the first great battle occurred. There had been many minor engagements, to be sure, such as that at Rich Mountain, but in none of these had there been a serious test of strength between the two great battle forces. This is a little hard to understand, especially when Confederate soldiers were to be found within a few miles of Washington most of the time. The real reason, of course, was the fact that neither side was prepared for war. Armies had to be recruited and trained, and munitions had to be bought or manufactured. Money had to be obtained, and the people, on both sides, had to be aroused to the real meaning of the struggle before them.

A glance at the map on page 34 will show how close together were the two Capitals. Washington, on the Potomac, was only one hundred, eleven miles from Richmond on the James. From Washington, the Potomac River flowed down into Chesapeake Bay, and from Chesapeake Bay one might go by boat directly to the wharves of Richmond. This latter fact explains a great deal. It tells us why the Potomac River was so important, and why half-way towns, like Fredericksburg, were fought over so many times. It explains why both sides felt it so necessary to keep armies always on hand to prevent the other side from striking some deadly blow at the seat of government.

THE HOME OF ROBERT E. LEE
THE MILITARY GENIUS WHO DIRECTED THE CONFEDERATE FORCES

Between the District of Columbia and the Virginia shore runs the Potomac River. It is fairly broad where, on the opposite bank, rise up the noble heights of Arlington. Today, a National Cemetery covers the green rolling slopes, but in 1861, Arlington Heights was the property of Robert E. Lee and upon it stood his palatial mansion. At the time this photograph was taken, the estate had just been occupied by Federal soldiers. You see them standing guard before its majestic Doric pillars.

As you look at this beautiful house your mind's eye must run back, far into our nation's history, for the adopted son of George Washington built it as a tribute to his grandmother, Martha Washington. History was made in the shadow of its walls. Up these broad steps walked Lafayette and, in 1831, in the room to the left of the main hall, Robert E. Lee was married to the only daughter of the house, the daughter of George Washington's adopted son.

Today, the grounds of the old estate hold many thousands of honored dead and it is curious and interesting to note that the *first* of the many thousands to be laid to rest there was a soldier of the Confederacy.

10

MARSHALL HOUSE, ALEXANDRIA, IN 1861   COLONEL ELLSWORTH

Fort Sumter was fired upon in April, 1861. Between that date and early May, Alexandria, just across the river from Washington, was in the hands of the Confederate soldiers. On the 24th of May, Colonel Ephraim E. Ellsworth, the commander of the Fire Zouaves, led his men across the river and captured the Virginia city. He saw the flag of the Confederacy proudly floating over the Marshall House hotel. Halting his men before the door, he entered the crowded lobby and ran up the steps. With the flag in his hand, a moment later, he descended. "Behold my trophy!" he cried. "Behold mine!" shouted the hotel keeper as he raised a shotgun and emptied its charge into the young man's breast. In itself, this incident is of little importance in a war that cost the lives of hundreds of thousands of brave men, but the shooting shocked the entire North and stiffened its determination to wage war upon the South.

When the killing of the young officer was made known through the daily press, the people of the North began to bring terrific pressure to bear upon President Lincoln to do something to end this unfortunate state of affairs. Lincoln was a man of peace and he shrank from any action that might involve the nation in a deadly struggle. To understand his feeling one must remember that many of the leaders on both sides were close, personal friends. Some of them had worked together in Washington. Others had been closely associated in the Army and Navy. It did not seem possible that a war, in which thousands should die, *could* be fought between people who had so much in common. All during the first anxious months of the struggle, people on both sides hoped and prayed that nothing would happen, on a large scale, that would prevent the trouble from being settled by peaceful means.

A BLOCKHOUSE BUILT TO DEFEND THE RAILROAD AGAINST RAIDS

The Confederate troops were so close to Washington during the early months of the war that the Federal Commander, Winfield Scott, deemed it necessary to build blockhouses on Arlington Heights to protect the Capital against surprise attacks and insure the safety of the water supply that flowed down over Aqueduct Bridge from the Virginia hills. These blockhouses were built of heavy logs. As forts, they did not amount to much, but, nevertheless, each housed two cannons, and each had loopholes cut through the walls for the use of the riflemen within. A few well-directed shells from a Confederate battery would have leveled these houses, but such shells were never fired. Even while sentries paced the farther bank of the Potomac, there was a feeling that, somehow or other, a means of avoiding further bloodshed would be found. Each side was unwilling to begin a war that all knew would be waged with terrible bitterness, once it had begun. Thus it happened that, all through the summer and fall of 1861, sentries faced each other without firing a shot. Both sides were marking time. Armies had to be created. In Washington, men were being enlisted for three months of service. They were being hastily drilled and armed. In and around Richmond, the Confederate Generals were equally busy building one of the world's bravest and most determined armies.

THIS BLOCKHOUSE DEFENDED AQUEDUCT BRIDGE, ARLINGTON HEIGHTS

BUILDING THE BARRICADES AT ALEXANDRIA AS A PROTECTION AGAINST CONFEDERATE CAVALRY RAIDS

Not far from Alexandria, the horsemen of the South rode without fear. Now and then, in a wild burst of fury, they raided far into Federal territory, destroying railroads and overturning engines and cars. In these raids, conducted with great swiftness and thoroughness, the Confederate Cavalry not only kept its leaders informed of what was taking place beyond the lines but captured much-needed food supplies. Many times, the sound of firing could be heard in Alexandria and, after the battle of Bull Run, the inhabitants lived in such a state of terror that they hastily built barricades strong enough to withstand the rush of cavalry. Behind these barricades the Federal forces waited, not knowing when the clatter and roar of charging horses would resound along the streets of the little town.

A STOCKADE GUARDING ONE OF THE STREETS

13

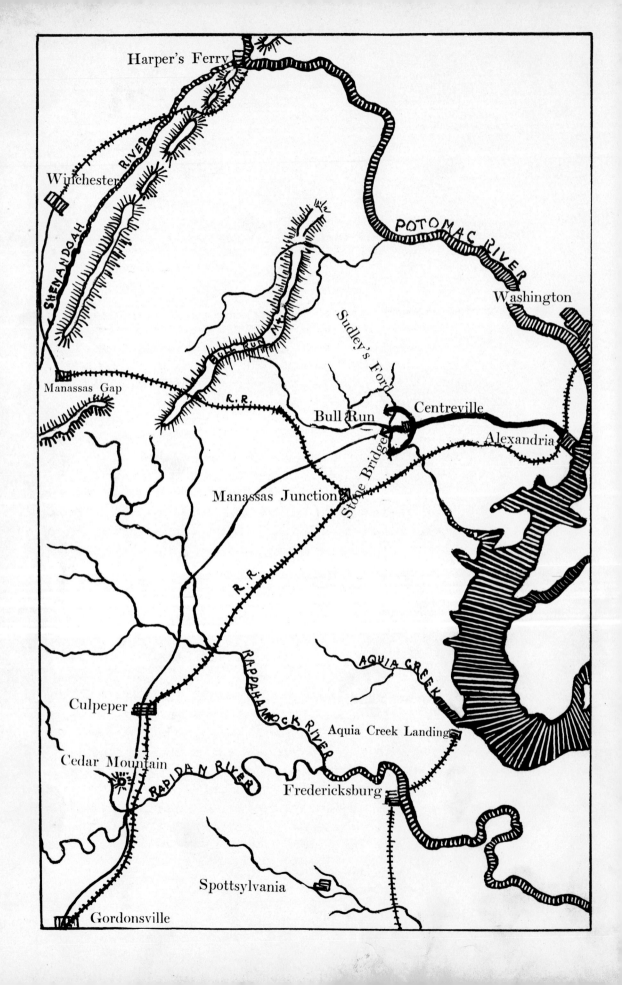

MANASSAS JUNCTION (BULL RUN) FOR WHICH THE BATTLE WAS FOUGHT

Railroad centers have always been the object of attack by opposing forces. This was as true in the days of the Civil War as it is today. The chief railroad center south of Washington was Manassas Junction. At that point two roads came together before they entered the City of Alexandria. From the beginning of the war this Junction was in the hands of the Confederates, and over the railroads that led up from Richmond they carried great quantities of supplies for the army near Washington. It was, indeed, a valuable position for either army to hold, and it is no wonder that, when the Federal forces marched out to the attack, the Confederates rallied around this spot and fought desperately to keep it. Because the battle raged along the banks of Bull Run Creek, it became known to history as the Battle of Bull Run.

There were in fact *two* battles of Bull Run,—the one we are about to study and the one fought a year later. Both are equally important, since on the outcome of both depended the security of the National Capital. After the *first* battle of Bull Run, the depot remained in the hands of the Confederate soldiers until General McClellan made plans to start down the Potomac to attack Richmond. It was then given up and the Federal troops immediately made it a supply base. The quantity of supplies piled up near the station attracted the attention of "Stonewall" Jackson, and, with twenty thousand men, he made a remarkable forced march and captured it. This battle took place on the 26th of August 1862.

This picture shows the condition of the station just after it fell into Confederate hands after this *second* battle. General Gordon, who was a witness, describes the scene as follows: "Here, a yellow-haired, barefooted son of the South claimed as prizes a toothbrush, a box of candies, and a barrel of coffee, while another, whose butternut homespun hung around him in tatters, crammed himself with lobster salad, sardines, potted game, and sweetmeats, and washed them down with Rhenish wine. Nor was the outer man neglected. From piles of new clothing, the Southerners arrayed themselves in the blue uniforms of the Federals. The naked were clad, the barefooted were shod and the sick provided with luxuries to which they had long been strangers." The capture was, as this quotation shows, a veritable boon for the Southern army.

MANASSAS JUNCTION AS IT APPEARED AFTER THE SECOND BATTLE
NOTE THE TURNTABLE IN THE FOREGROUND

ONE OF THE RAILROAD BRIDGES WRECKED DURING THE SECOND BATTLE

THE LITTLE VILLAGE OF CENTREVILLE, VIRGINIA
THE FIRST BATTLE OF BULL RUN IS ABOUT TO BEGIN

All through the night of July 20th, 1861, and long into the early morning hours of the 21st, lines of slowly-moving Federal troops marched steadily past this old stone church at Centreville, Virginia. They had crossed the Potomac River two days before and were on their way to capture Manassas Junction, a spot that was destined to live forever in American memory as the place where the battle of Bull Run was fought.

The uniforms of these men were new and their muskets glinted in the moonlight or shone brightly in the early morning sun. These men marched as though they were on their way to a picnic. Some dropped out of line to pick flowers, while others sat down now and then to rest themselves. They did not expect any serious opposition and, so strong was the feeling in Washington that the Confederate cause would go down swiftly before the march of these raw recruits, that thousands of people packed lunches and drove out to the Confederate lines to see the power of the South broken forever.

The men who marched had never faced an enemy in battle. They knew little of the art of war. They had not had time to learn. They were marching this bright morning in July because the press and the people of the North, tired of marking time, were clamoring for action. Upon these marching men had been thrust the duty of driving an armed menace from the vicinity of Washington.

THESE TROOPS CROSSED THE FORD SHOWN IN THE PICTURE BELOW. THEY WERE A SMALL PART OF THE FORCE SENT TO TURN THE LEFT OF THE CONFEDERATE ARMY

General McDowell, who commanded the Federal forces, had worked out a careful plan of attack. He halted his center before the stone bridge and sent his right divisions to cross Bull Run at a spot known as Sudley Ford. These men were instructed to cross the ford and then work down along the banks of the river to the stone bridge. They were surprised to find their crossing of the ford unopposed.

SUDLEY FORD WHERE VICTORY SEEMED CERTAIN FOR THE FEDERAL SOLDIERS

**THIS IS BULL RUN AS IT APPEARED THE MORNING OF THE BATTLE
THE WORD "RUN" IS ANOTHER NAME FOR CREEK**

Armies have always found streams and swamps valuable aids in holding off an enemy. From this picture we can get a very true impression of the difficulties that faced the Federal soldiers when they reached the banks of Bull Run. With enemy sharpshooters, many of whom were experienced hunters, hidden in the thickets and behind trees on the opposite shore, any attempt to force the stream by throwing across trunks of trees or wading or swimming would have meant certain death to large numbers of attackers. The Northern Generals knew this only too well and their plan of battle did not include any such desperate efforts. It happened that there was a sturdy stone bridge on the main road out of Centreville that crossed Bull Run at a spot where there were few trees. It was towards this bridge that the center of the Federal troops marched. When the men came within gunshot of this bridge they halted, much to the surprise of the Confederates who expected an immediate assault.

THE STONE BRIDGE AT BULL RUN

**THE KIND OF MEN WHO MARCHED THROUGH THE VILLAGE OF CENTREVILLE
THE THIRD CONNECTICUT REGIMENT**

As they marched, these men sang and shouted, "On to Richmond!" An ugly rumor had, however, spread through the ranks, going from man to man, down the long, swaying lines. "Two days before," so said this rumor, "a scouting party of Federal troops had reached Blackburn's Ford on Bull Run, not far from where they marched, and had there met the enemy in a fierce battle that left nineteen Federal dead upon the field." Perhaps these men of the South were *not* to be so easily defeated as everyone had prophesied.

In this case, Rumor had been correct. In the picture below, we see the exact spot where this first battle occurred. The picture was taken a year later, during the period when the Federal troops had come into possession of Manassas Station. The picture is introduced at this point, since it presents an excellent view of Bull Run and gives us our first glimpse of the pontoon bridge,—a device, for crossing streams, that was to play a vital part in the later history of the war. At this spot, the valley of Bull Run spreads out into a pleasant level area. For the most part, the stream runs between high, wooded banks, with many swampy places intervening, where men and horses bog down to their knees.

BLACKBURN'S FORD WHERE THE FIRST SKIRMISH OF THE BATTLE TOOK PLACE

AT THIS STONE BRIDGE THE FEDERAL SOLDIERS WAITED
THEY WERE NOT TO CROSS UNTIL THEIR COMRADES CAME DOWN THE OTHER SIDE

The Confederate officers became worried when the Federal soldiers did not try to cross the stone bridge. They sent scouts on fast horses up and down the stream to find out what the delay meant. At last they saw a cloud of dust rising above the trees far upstream. This cloud of dust told them the entire story of the Federal attempt to cross at Sudley Ford and come down on their left flank and rear. The Confederate Generals were skilful men. They withdrew from the stone bridge at once and placed their army on a ridge that ran along the stream. At advantageous spots they wheeled up batteries of heavy guns, and then waited for the Federal soldiers to appear.

They hastily threw up breastworks made of trees and hid themselves behind rocks and stumps. The cannon they had drawn up covered the opening into which they knew the Federal troops would advance on their way down the stream to the stone bridge. They did not have long to wait. A blue line began to surge forward, like a wave, out of the forest beyond. Guns roared on both sides and the first great battle of the Civil War was under way. The Federal soldiers recoiled from the terrible fire that was poured upon them. They quickly reformed their lines and charged again and again.

THORNTON'S HOUSE—AROUND THIS HOUSE RAGED THE BATTLE OF BULL RUN

It was here that the men who crossed at Sudley Ford first came into actual contact with the forces of the South. This peaceful scene, taken just before the battle, gives us little idea of the fury with which the storm of war broke over it a few hours later. An officer's horse is seen tied to the fence rail and children are watching the photographer as he works. Even as they watched, the tides of war were rolling in from both sides to engulf the spot.

Below are shown the first to die on the great battle field of Bull Run. We cannot tell from the picture whether they belong to the blue or the gray. We only know that they were brave men who fought and died for a cause in which they sincerely believed.

During this terrible battle, the Federals lost four hundred and eighty-one killed and two thousand, four hundred wounded or missing. The Confederate loss was three hundred, seventy-eight killed and fourteen hundred wounded. Some of the missing, on the Federal side, can be accounted for by the departure of many three month volunteers, whose term of enlistment expired on that very day and who simply left the battlefield and went home.

NEVER AGAIN TO LOOK UPON THE SUN

WHERE THE CONFEDERATES WAVERED AND THEN FLED

Just north of this house the Confederate Colonel, Evans, met the advancing columns of Burnside and Porter. A furious battle began at once and raged all through the morning hours. The fire on both sides was so intense that men fell in ghastly heaps as the soldiers charged to the attack. About noon the Confederates began to give way. The battle now raged around this old stone house. Men crouched behind the rail fence and fought from behind the trees. At last, the situation became so desperate, for the Confederate cause, that the leaders, Johnston and Beauregard, galloped to the scene at full speed. They arrived in the vicinity of the stone house about noon. Their soldiers were falling back in disorder. They tried to rally them, but at that moment a charge of fresh Federal troops swept up the hill.

One General in the Confederate ranks saw the danger. He advanced with a battery to the ridge just behind the Robinson House shown below. It was his purpose to hold back the charging Federals until General Bee, who commanded the Confederate soldiers, could rally them in his rear. General Bee, sitting on his charger under the trees in front of this house, saw General Jackson make his stand. Reaching out his arm towards the artillery brigade, he cried, "Look at Jackson, standing there like a stone wall!" As he spoke, a bullet struck him and he fell forward on his horse's neck crying, "Rally the Virginians!"

NOT FAR FROM THIS HOUSE "STONEWALL" JACKSON WON ETERNAL FAME

THE SPINNER HOUSE WAS TURNED INTO A HOSPITAL

We must now turn back to the old stone bridge for the concluding chapter in this savage battle. At three o'clock that afternoon, just as the Federal forces were rejoicing in the thought that they had won a great victory, a faint cheering was heard from the Confederate ranks far across the hills. The cheering grew louder and louder. Soon marching columns of Confederate soldiers were seen advancing to renew the battle. A shout went up from the front ranks that echoed and re-echoed along the Virginia hills. "Johnston has come! Johnston has come!"

At that moment, Johnston was supposed to be at Winchester, far from the scene of battle. As a matter of fact he had come to Manassas Junction two days before with two thirds of his army. What the weary Federal soldiers saw, as the despairing cry ran along their ranks, was the other third of Johnston's army. It had been rushed from Winchester by rail to Manassas Junction and was now swinging into battle, fresh from a long rest.

The weary soldiers of the North, thinking that Johnston's entire army of thousands of men had come down upon their flank and rear, broke into a disorderly retreat. It must be remembered that they were poorly trained and entirely unversed in the art of war. The retreat grew into a panic, and soon the roads back to Washington were thronged, not only with retreating soldiers, but with hundreds of sight-seers who had come so bravely forth to see the might of the South destroyed forever.

Past this old house rushed the frenzied throng. Within its walls lay wounded Federal soldiers. In the rear, pressed the Confederate cavalry. At this spot, a Congressman and a large number of sight-seers and soldiers were captured.

Back to Washington fled the discouraged troops, carrying with them the sad

Photo by U. S. Army Signal Corps

A FORD ON BULL RUN SPANNED BY A PONTOON BRIDGE

news of disaster. Would the Confederate Generals press their victory home? Would they follow the defeated soldiers into Washington, itself? No one knew. Everyone hoped that, somehow, the broad Potomac would check the rush of the victorious armies of the South. In the hearts of the leaders at Washington grew, almost overnight, a sense of the importance of the struggle that had so disastrously begun.

Almost before the last straggler had reached the Capital, steps were being taken to raise a new army and, so thoroughly train it and equip it, that the next battle would tell a different story.

The failure of the Confederates to follow up their great victory is very hard, even in this day, to understand. "Having won the completest victory of modern times," said one military expert, "they set to work to fortify themselves for defense

25

WOODEN MARKERS FOR THE MEN WHO FELL IN THIS SPOT

against the enemy they had so disastrously overthrown, precisely as if they had been beaten in the fight, and were called upon to defend themselves against an enemy to be feared." Whatever may have been the reason, the Confederates lost, at this spot, their one great chance of victory. The speed with which the Southern troops threw up the breastworks shown in these pictures alarmed the leaders in Washington. Never from that day until Manassas Junction was once more in its hands, did the Federal Government dare to leave Washington without the guarding strength of thousands of soldiers. Time and again, when men were needed to press on to victory, those men were encamped behind the fortifications that watched over the Capital. The necessity for thus guarding the City of Washington had much to do also with the delays that set in,—delays which became the cause of so much discontent in the North that President Lincoln was at last compelled to ask General McClellan, who had now been placed in command, to make some forward move to defeat the forces of the Confederacy.

DUMMY GUNS SET UP IN THE HOPE THAT THEY WOULD DISCOURAGE THE FEDERALS

INSTEAD OF FOLLOWING UP THEIR VICTORY THE CONFEDERATES WAITED

**CONFEDERATE ENTRENCHMENTS AT CENTREVILLE ERECTED AFTER THE FIRST BATTLE
OF BULL RUN**

THE FEDERAL ARMY BEING DRILLED NEAR WASHINGTON

DRUMMER BOYS. SOME ARE LESS THAN FIFTEEN YEARS OF AGE

THE JAMES RIVER IN 1862. THIS PICTURE WAS TAKEN NEAR DREWRY'S BLUFF AND SHOWS THE SHIPS SUNK IN THE RIVER TO KEEP THE "MONITOR" FROM ATTACKING RICHMOND

CHAPTER TWO

THE PENINSULAR CAMPAIGN OF 1862

The Battle of the "Monitor" and the "Merrimac"

Before we can take up the work of the armies of the Federal Government and follow them as they struck southward into Virginia by way of the Potomac River and Chesapeake Bay we must consider the part the navy played in making possible this attempt to capture the Southern Capital. From the time Fort Sumter was fired on, the Confederate commanders had control of the Virginia shore of the Potomac River. This control extended from a short distance below Alexandria down the waters of the Potomac, across its mouth to Norfolk and thence southward to Florida and along the gulf to the mouth of the Mississippi River. Before any attack could be made by water against Richmond, this situation had to be changed. During the early months of the war, a blockade was established along the coast to prevent the South from getting supplies from across the seas. In August, General Butler captured two forts at Hatteras Inlet. In November, General Sherman and Admiral Dupont took possession of the forts at Port Royal in South Carolina. By the end of April, the Federal banner was flying over Fort Macon, Beaufort Harbor, North Carolina. It was about this time that the *Merrimac* was seen from Fortress Monroe. On March 8th, this reconditioned ship, equipped by the Confederates

THE BATTLE BETWEEN THE "MONITOR" AND THE "MERRIMAC" HAMPTON ROADS, MARCH 9TH, 1862

THIS IS AN ARTIST'S CONCEPTION. COMPARE THE "MONITOR" IN THIS PICTURE WITH THE ORIGINAL "MONITOR" AS SHOWN IN THE PHOTOGRAPH ON THE OPPOSITE PAGE

THE "CHEESE BOX" THAT MADE HISTORY AS IT APPEARED FOUR MONTHS AFTER THE BATTLE

with thick, armor-plated sides, appeared in Hampton Roads and destroyed, in a few hours, two of the Federal vessels,—the *Congress* and the *Cumberland*. From her thick, iron-covered sides, the shot of the Federal war vessels bounced like peas. There was the greatest anxiety among the Northern naval officers as night set in and put an end to the unequal fight. It was apparent that the *Merrimac* had come through the battle without serious damage. It would be impossible to describe the thrill of joy that swept through the South at the news of this victory. It meant breaking the blockade that was slowly strangling the Confederacy. It meant food and supplies of all kinds from over seas. Meanwhile, in the North, there was the utmost dismay.

It happened, however, that the Federal Government had heard rumors of the building of a strange, armored craft, and, in order to meet its menace, had turned to the design of a similar vessel submitted some time before by one of its own employees, a man named John Ericsson. This man had laid a plan before the authorities covering the building of an armored ship, with a revolving turret in which guns could be mounted.

Ericsson's plan had been approved and this strange ship, nicknamed by those who first saw it, a "Cheese Box," was actually on its trial run at the very moment

31

THE CREW AT EASE. THESE MEN, SHOWN HERE AT REST, PLAYING CHECKERS AND READING LETTERS, HAD A SHORT TIME BEFORE, FEARLESSLY FOUGHT THE "MERRIMAC" ON DECEMBER 31. MANY OF THEM WENT DOWN WITH THE "MONITOR" WHEN SHE FOUNDERED OFF HATTERAS

the *Merrimac* was spreading havoc among the ships of the fleet in Hampton Roads. As a matter of fact, her commander saw the smoke of the blazing *Congress* as she passed along the coast and he at once made for the scene of the conflict with all speed.

When daylight came, the *Merrimac* returned to finish the work she had begun. She made straight for the *Minnesota* with the intention of sinking her as quickly as possible. In the night, however, the *Monitor* had placed herself alongside the *Minnesota* and, as the first guns roared, she slipped out and swung into a position directly in front of the *Merrimac*. She seemed, to those who watched, like a pigmy about to attack a giant. What she lacked in size, however, was more than made up in power. Her guns blazed, as her shot-proof turret began slowly to revolve. The *Merrimac* trained her guns on the midget war vessel, but her biggest shot bounded off the iron sides. The battle raged for some time. Neither antagonist could gain any advantage. The *Merrimac* now saw that it was useless to waste shot and

THE CREW OF THE "MONITOR" PREPARES A MEAL ON DECK

any advantage. The *Merrimac* now saw that it was useless to waste shot and powder on the *Monitor*, so she turned her guns upon the *Minnesota*. Immediately the gunners of the smaller craft sent shot after shot against the *Merrimac*. One heavy ball pierced its armor and did damage to the interior. The *Merrimac* now tried to ram the *Monitor* but was more damaged in the crash than the smaller vessel. Suddenly, the guns, as though at some invisible signal, ceased firing on both sides. The *Monitor* turned and steamed slowly away towards Fortress Monroe, while the *Merrimac*, with her tenders, started in the direction of Norfolk.

Thus ended, not only the battle between the great ironclads, but also the menace of the ironclad itself so far as the North was concerned. With its superior ship building yards and abundance of materials, the North was in a position to outstrip its antagonist in any vessel-building race.

The *Merrimac* never again became a serious menace. After the evacuation of Norfolk, May 9th, 1862, she was blown up to prevent her falling into Northern hands. The *Monitor*, on December 31st, 1862, foundered in a terrific storm and carried two officers and twelve men to the bottom with her. The battle of these two ironclads proved to the world the usefulness of armor as a protection for ships of war.

With the control of the rivers and coastal areas in its grasp, the North was now ready to begin the invasion of the South by way of the Potomac River and Chesapeake Bay.

33

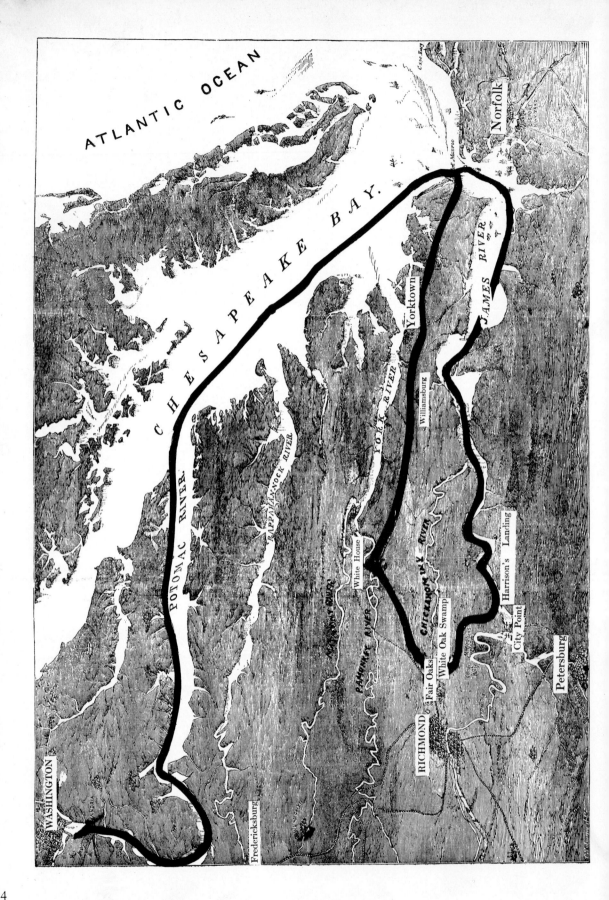

ATLANTIC OCEAN

CHESAPEAKE BAY.

Norfolk

JAMES RIVER

Yorktown

Williamsburg

YORK RIVER

POTOMAC RIVER.

RAPPAHANNOCK RIVER

MATTAPONI RIVER.

PAMUNKEY RIVER.

White House

CHICKAHOMINY RIVER

Harrison's Landing

City Point

RICHMOND

Fair Oaks
White Oak Swamp

Petersburg

Fredericksburg

WASHINGTON

34

OVER THIS HOUSE, IN WHICH CORNWALLIS AGREED TO THE TERMS OF HIS SURRENDER, FLEW THE SHELLS OF THE NORTHERN BATTERIES

CHAPTER THREE

THE SIEGE OF YORKTOWN

As the winter months went by, the people of the North became more and more restless. Everyone knew that only thirty miles from Washington, at Manassas Junction, lay the Confederate army, with victory shining on its banners after the disaster of Bull Run. At last the 8th of March, 1862, arrived. As President Lincoln gazed across the Potomac on the morning of that historic day, he saw columns of smoke rising from the southwest. The Confederate General Johnston was abandoning his camp at Manassas Junction. He had heard rumors that the army of the Potomac was about to move, by way of the river, to Chesapeake Bay, and he had no desire to find himself suddenly cut off from Richmond. Thus it came about that a simple military maneuver accomplished, without bloodshed, what an army had not been able to achieve, a year before, on the battlefield of Bull Run.

McClellan had at last decided to invade the South by way of the Potomac and Yorktown was his destination as he hurried his men and equipment aboard four hundred transports on the 17th of March, 1862.

The landing, near Fortress Monroe, was made under terrible weather conditions. The sea was rough and great billows broke with a thundering roar upon the beach. All through that rain swept night the troops went ashore as best they could and huddled together in the darkness. When the order to march came, they slogged forward to some open fields where they camped, with neither tents nor fire to protect and comfort them.

The Confederate Capital was seventy miles away. The path of march towards it, lay along the peninsula that stretched away from the sea between the York and the James Rivers. This peninsula was marshy and covered with thick woods, with many small tidal streams cutting through it.

THE CONFEDERATES STRENGTHENED THIS RAMPART WITH PRECIOUS BALES OF COTTON

On the afternoon of April 5th, 1862, the Federal advance guard came to the banks of the Warwick River. It was a slow, sluggish stream, easily crossed, but, on its western bank, defending the little village of Yorktown, could be seen lines of entrenchments, behind which waited Confederate soldiers. An attack was made, in which men waded across the stream holding their guns over their heads. The attack was beaten off so easily and with such heavy losses that General McClellan decided to capture Yorktown before moving on towards the Confederate Capital. This, of course, was just what the Southern Generals wanted. Richmond lay within striking distance. Its defences were none too strong. The siege of Yorktown, if it could be made to last a month, would give the Confederates the chance to build such formidable fortifications that no army could hope to take them by storm.

IT WAS HERE THAT McCLELLAN SET HIS HEADQUARTERS FOR THE ATTACK ON YORKTOWN

36

THESE TREMENDOUS GUNS WERE CALLED "MORTARS" AND WERE SET UP TO SHELL
YORKTOWN

BEHIND SUCH FORTIFICATIONS AS THESE THE FEDERAL FORCES FELT SAFE FROM ATTACK

37

GUNS OF THE NORTH

GUNS OF THE SOUTH

IT WAS THROUGH THIS OPENING, CALLED A SALLYPORT, THAT THE CONFEDERATES RETREATED

On the night of May 3d, 1862, after delaying the Federal forces for more than a month, the Confederate army withdrew from Yorktown. Most of the huge guns, that took so much time to set up, were never fired. The road, shown in the picture above, leads out onto the Williamsburg Highway. On that bright Sunday morning it roared with the rush of pursuing Federal cavalry. Six miles from Williamsburg, the rear of the retreating army was overtaken. A bitter battle took place. Darkness fell, as the main body of the Federal forces reached the scene. The fields in which these tired soldiers were compelled to spend the night were water-soaked and muddy.

The following day, the battle began again. Once more night fell. Meanwhile, it had begun to rain heavily. Through the darkness and storm, the Confederate soldiers made their way towards Richmond. They left their dead and wounded half buried in the mud. There was no time to do more than hastily care for those who fell in the line of march. Williamsburg lay ahead. Through its quaint streets soon sounded the heavy tread of men, marching in a steady stream, as the Army of the Potomac followed closely on the heels of the Confederate forces.

THE PEOPLE OF YORKTOWN GATHERED TO SEE THE FEDERAL TROOPS MARCH IN

THE WHARF AT YORKTOWN BECAME A BUSY SUPPLY DEPOT FOR THE FEDERAL FORCES

With Yorktown and Williamsburg behind it, the Army of the Potomac took up its march towards the Confederate Capital on the James River. Its route lay along the Pamunkey River. It was the 16th of May, however, before the advance corps reached "White House," the ancient home of the Lee family. In this old house McClellan took up his quarters.

Panic had seized the Confederate Capital. No one had dreamed that a Federal force could come within such short distance of Richmond. General Johnston, the Commander of the Southern forces, was not worried. He had achieved his purpose. He had delayed the advance of McClellan. Between his well-entrenched army and the Federals, lay the Chickahominy River,—a sluggish stream whose banks were lined with wooded swamps. In *dry* weather it was but a brook but, *now*, it was swollen with torrential rains.

CONFEDERATE CANNON OVERLOOKING THE JAMES RIVER—A MIGHTY REASON WHY RICHMOND WAS NOT THREATENED BY THE GUNBOATS OF THE FEDERAL NAVY

IN THE PICTURE BELOW, MAY BE SEEN THE BEAUTIFUL JAMES RIVER AS IT FLOWS TO THE SEA. HIGH ON ITS BANKS WERE LOCATED, IN MANY PLACES, POWERFUL CONFEDERATE BATTERIES

41

CUMBERLAND LANDING ON THE PAMUNKEY RIVER WHERE McCLELLAN HAD ESTABLISHED HIS HEADQUARTERS

A glance at the map on page 34 will show the position of "White House", on the Pamunkey River. Just below headquarters was Cumberland Landing where the troops were made as comfortable as possible during a period of heavy rains. In the picture above, we see the encampment stretching out as far as eye can follow. It is evening and the many campfires are filling the air with a soft haze. The soldiers in the foreground are, no doubt, talking over the days to come. Richmond, the object of their long and dangerous journey, lies only a few miles to the south. Little did these men, sitting there in the gathering twilight, anticipate the sufferings and defeats that lay ahead of them in the treacherous swamps that stretched between them and the Confederate Capital. Bridges were being built and roads constructed. They, themselves, that very day, had worked hard preparing the path over which they would tread on the morrow. Beyond the swollen waters of the Chickahominy, waited the Southern forces. That there would be a fierce battle no one doubted.

Meanwhile, the people of both North and South waited for the outcome in an agony of suspense.

THE SOLDIERS ARE LAYING DOWN LOGS TO MAKE A ROAD FOR THE GUNS

CHAPTER FOUR

ON TO RICHMOND!

From the army base at White House down to the Chickahominy, the ground was so soft that roads had to be built before the bridge ends could be reached. In this picture we see how this was done. The soldiers are laying logs side by side and holding them in place with deeply driven stakes. This type of road, known as "corduroy", proved most useful later on, when, without swift skill in its construction, the Army of the Potomac might have been totally destroyed.

The picture below shows one of the most famous of these roads. It was known as the "Grapevine" from the way it twisted here and there as it crossed the swamp.

THIS ROAD, MADE OF TREES CUT FROM THE NEIGHBORING SWAMP, WAS HASTILY BUILT
TO PERMIT PASSAGE OF MEN AND GUNS

43

ONE OF THE HASTILY CONSTRUCTED BRIDGES THAT McCLELLAN THREW ACROSS THE RIVER

On the night of May 30th, the swollen Chickahominy had swept away most of the hastily constructed bridges. Some of the artillery had been dragged across, but the marshy soil was so full of water and so soft that it became practically impossible to bring up the guns needed for the next day's battle. During the night of the 31st, Pettit's command managed, after superhuman effort, to drag their cannon up from the river bank to a position on the right of the Federal lines. The picture shown below gives us a wonderful view of the condition of these pieces of artillery, after they had finally been wheeled into position. These were the only big guns that arrived in time to take part in the battle that was about to be fought.

The Williamsburg stage road crossed the Chickahominy at Bottom's Bridge, eleven miles from Richmond. It was along this road that one of the divisions made its way.

THESE GUNS SHOW PLAINLY THE TERRIBLE ROAD CONDITIONS ENCOUNTERED

44

FAIR OAKS FARM . . . THE FIELD OF DEATH

CHAPTER FIVE

The Battle of Fair Oaks or Seven Pines

Seven miles from Richmond, where another road cuts across the Williamsburg Highway, grew seven pines. A thousand yards beyond these pines were two farm houses, known through the countryside as Fair Oaks Farm. Since the battle raged beneath these pines and around these houses, it is known to history as the Battle of Fair Oaks or Seven Pines.

The night before the battle was one of terror for the soldiers on both sides. The most violent storm that had ever swept the region burst over their heads. The sky was continuously lit with lightning and the rain fell in such torrents that no shelter could keep it out. The lowlands became lakes, and, the next morning the battle raged back and forth for hours, now one side getting the advantage, now the other. The soldiers moved to battle through mud that was in places ankle deep.

The picture shown above was taken immediately after one of the most terrible assaults. Over four hundred men died at this spot and their hastily dug graves can be clearly seen in the foreground. The redoubt, just beyond the houses, was the very center of the Federal lines. By looking closely, far in the rear, one may see General Sickle's Brigade drawn up in line of battle.

The picture at the bottom of this page tells a most interesting story. On the afternoon of May 31st, the Confederates were fiercely driving the Federal troops before them. This battery, under the command of an officer named Murphy, together with a battery commanded by Miller, opened fire with such deadly aim that the Confederates were halted and time given the Federals to reform. The guns of this battery grew so hot that, only with the greatest care, could they we swabbed out and reloaded. This battery of brave and determined men was known as Company C, 1st Pennsylvania Artillery.

THE DEADLY FIRE OF THIS BATTERY HALTED THE ON-RUSHING CONFEDERATES

45

"CEASE FIRING!"

The result of the *first* day's fighting at Fair Oaks was, without doubt, a Federal defeat and might have been turned into a retreat had not General Sumner, crossing his troops on the perilous "Grapevine" bridge shown in a preceding picture, come up in time to rally the wavering soldiers. The results of the *second* day's action was more favorable for the Federal soldiers and the Confederates were driven back upon Richmond.

The picture shown above gives us a glimpse of the Federal artillerymen just at the moment they have received the order to cease firing. Several of the gunners may be observed in the act of sighting the guns just before firing them.

The Battle of Fair Oaks is of special importance in our study of the Civil War, not so much because of the fact that it was the turning point in McClellan's Peninsular Campaign, but because of something else,—something far more important, that happened during the battle.

General Johnston had been placed in command of the Confederate forces at the beginning of the war. It was he who came onto the field of Bull Run just in time to turn defeat into victory for the South. He was an able General in many ways, but not the military genius that was needed, if the South were to have any hope of victory.

46

WHITE OAK SWAMP, WHERE THE MEN, STANDING WAIST DEEP IN WATER, FOUGHT WITH BAYONETS

During the first day of the battle of Fair Oaks General Johnston was struck by a rifle-ball, and, almost immediately, a shell hit him, knocking him from his horse. He was carried from the field in a desperate condition. Although the command for the next day's battle was entrusted to General G. W. Smith, Robert E. Lee was promoted to be the new leader of the Confederate forces. *The arrival of this man had more to do with prolonging the war than any other single cause.* Against his military genius the blows of the Federal forces were destined to fall in vain for many weary months.

47

THE FARMHOUSES, SHOWN ON THIS PAGE, STOOD ON THE BATTLEFIELD AND WERE CONVERTED INTO HOSPITALS. THE NUMBER OF WOUNDED WAS SO GREAT THAT TENTS WERE PUT UP IN WHICH THE LESS SERIOUS CASES WERE GIVEN CARE

The effect of Lee's advancement was at once apparent. Lee considered that the time had come to take the offensive and drive the Federals from the vicinity of Richmond. As a result of the seven days of battle that followed, McClellan was forced from one position to another in a retreat that was finally to come to an end under the guns of the Federal navy on the James River.

UNDER SUCH CONDITIONS AS THESE, SHATTERED ARMS AND LEGS WERE CUT OFF. OFTEN THE SOLDIERS DID NOT EVEN HAVE THE AID OF CHLOROFORM TO DEADEN THEIR SUFFERINGS

Following the battle of Fair Oaks, the Confederate army fell back upon its entrenchments. At this time, the Federal forces were within six miles of Richmond and the Northern fleet had steamed up the James River to within eight miles of the Capital of the Confederacy. The fleet was halted at this point by the fire of batteries located on Drewry's Bluff, a picture of which will be found on page 29. McClellan's confidence in his ability to take Richmond had begun to waver. His army had been terribly weakened by disease and gun fire. The conditions under which each battle was fought were the worst that could be imagined, and the skill with which General Lee anticipated every move cast dark shadows over the hopes of the entire North.

MECHANICSVILLE, WHERE THE FEDERAL ARMY WAS HALTED IN ITS TRACKS

McClellan's decision to abandon the Peninsular Campaign was hastened by what happened at Mechanicsville. In the picture above, the photographer has given us a beautiful glimpse of this sleepy little village on that historic day when the Federal army, attempting to occupy the town, was defeated and driven back, with heavy losses. While this victory, in itself, was of very minor importance, it filled the South with the wildest joy, and so increased the confidence and morale of the Confederate soldiers that, from that day forth, they held firm against any further advances by McClellan's regiments.

Before making any further move towards Richmond, McClellan decided to wait for reinforcements from Washington. He entrenched his men behind strong barricades not far from the battlefield of Fair Oaks. The weeks went by. Richmond was but five miles away. The country wondered, and President Lincoln grew more and more disturbed and restless. In spite of the pressure, McClellan never moved. He spent his time drilling his men to a pitch of perfection that he thought would insure victory. Meanwhile, in the west, a new military light was rising. General Grant was winning victories while McClellan waited within the shadows of the Capital of the Confederacy.

The forces of Lee were not idle. Attack after attack kept the Federal soldiers constantly in action. Supply depots were raided. Swiftly moving cavalry units descended with lightning speed, attacked and disappeared. At last, McClellan decided to give up the siege of Richmond and retire to a spot on the James River where he would have the support of the Federal gunboats.

AT THIS SPOT McCLELLAN WAITED FOR REINFORCEMENTS AND SUPPLIES

SAVAGE'S STATION, WHERE BITTER BATTLES WERE FOUGHT FOR FEDERAL SUPPLIES

Allen's farmhouse, shown in the picture, stands just back from the Williamsburg Road over which McClellan moved most of his supplies. Confederate raiders repeatedly attacked this position in the hope of capturing vast quantities of materials so much needed for their own army. In spite of the speed with which McClellan transferred his men to new positions on the James, cars loaded with food and ammunition had to be abandoned. These were run at full speed off the end of the ruined bridge shown in the picture below.

McCLELLAN, IN ORDER TO PREVENT THEIR CAPTURE BY THE CONFEDERATES, RAN CARS LOADED WITH SUPPLIES INTO THE RIVER AT THIS POINT

51

WOUNDED CONFEDERATE SOLDIERS PICKED UP AFTER THE BATTLE OF SAVAGE'S STATION

An eminent authority, in writing about this strange retreat, says this:

McClellan's one hope, one purpose, was to march his army out of the swamps and escape from the ceaseless Confederate assaults to a point on the James River where the resistless fire of the gunboats might protect his men from further attacks and give them a chance to rest. To that end he retreated night and day, standing at bay now and then as the hunted stag does, and fighting desperately for the poor privilege of running away.—Eggleston.

In his swift retreat, McClellan finally reached Malvern Heights, a high plateau, overlooking the James River. Here, he turned and met the assaults of the enemy. His position was not only naturally strong but was protected by many pieces of heavy and light artillery and by the fire of the gunboats lying at anchor in the river below. The results of the battle were all in favor of the Federal army. The Confederate forces had shattered their might in costly attacks on positions that could not be taken. In the night, however, in spite of the brave protests of such fellow generals as Kearney and Hooker, McClellan ordered a retreat to Harrison's Landing on the southern shore of the James River. This action aroused terrific protests in the North, where many people began to suspect that General McClellan was either a traitor or was lacking in those qualities of generalship so needed to win the war against such leadership as that of Robert E. Lee.

PROTECTED BY THE HEAVY GUNS OF THE FLEET, THE ARMY OF THE POTOMAC RESTED AT
HARRISON'S LANDING ON THE JAMES RIVER.   THESE PICTURES GIVE US A GLIMPSE OF THE
MANNER IN WHICH THE SOLDIERS WERE HOUSED AND FED.   IN THE PICTURE SHOWN ABOVE,
THE COOK IS ABOUT TO SLAUGHTER A COW FOR THE NOON MEAL.

DINNER TIME . . . FIRST MASSACHUSETTS LIGHT BATTERY

COOKING OUT OF DOORS WAS NO EASY TASK

FEDERAL ARTILLERY NOT FAR FROM CEDAR MOUNTAIN ON THE DAY OF BATTLE

These men, a short time later, were exposed to a terrific Confederate fire and suffered large losses. Before the rising of another sun two thousand of their comrades lay dead or wounded on the slopes of Cedar Mountain.

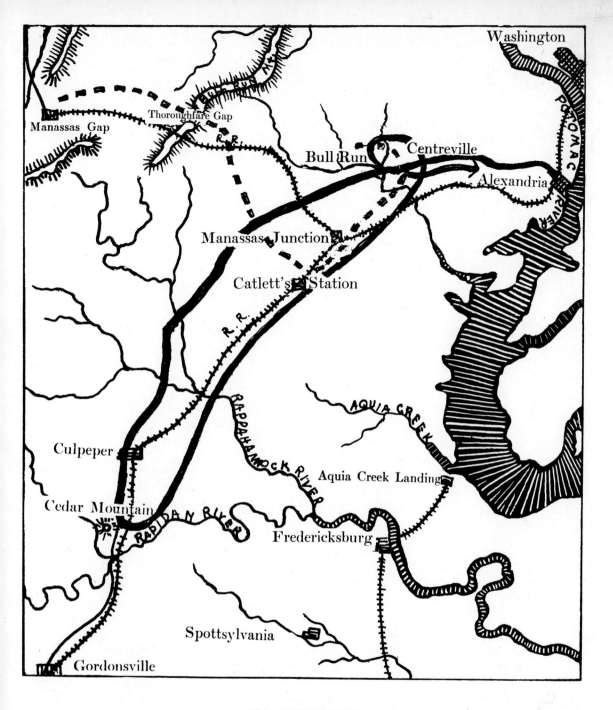

CHAPTER SIX

THE BATTLE OF CEDAR MOUNTAIN

General George B. McClellan had failed to capture Richmond. On the other hand, in the west, at Donelson, Pea Ridge, and Shiloh, the men in command had scored important victories. No one wondered, therefore, when President Lincoln summoned General Pope from the west to take command of the army he had speedily organized for the defense of Washington. General Pope had the reputation of hunting down his foe and destroying him without delay.

SUPPLY WAGONS ON THE MOVE. NOTE THE FORWARD ACTION IN THIS REMARKABLE PICTURE!

General Pope at once determined to push southward and occupy the important railroad junction of Gordonsville from whence he would be within striking distance by rail of Richmond, itself. He thought such a move would draw some of Lee's forces into the north and thus allow McClellan to escape, without heavy losses, from his uncertain position on the James River.

Lee, however, learning that McClellan was about to retreat from the James, had sent "Stonewall" Jackson to occupy Gordonsville. It was an important spot, that he could ill afford to lose.

On August 6th, 1862, Pope began his advance southward. The picture on page 54 gives a beautiful glimpse of his advance guard, as a cavalry unit stops to rest and water its horses.

The busiest men in the whole army were the engineers. It was their task to throw bridges across the North Branch of the Rappahannock River where, at Sulphur Springs, it halted the wagon trains and artillery.

A SPOT ON THE RAPPAHANNOCK RIVER PICKED OUT FOR ITS QUIET BEAUTY

IN AN HOUR SUPPLY WAGONS AND HEAVY GUNS WILL RUMBLE ACROSS THESE BRIDGES

THE HUDSON HOUSE WHERE POPE WAITED AS HIS ARMY ADVANCED ON GORDONSVILLE

Meanwhile Pope, advancing to the little village of Culpeper, set up his headquarters in the Hudson House. He had, meanwhile sent his army southward to seize Gordonsville. He was too late. Jackson had already seized the important railroad junction and was sweeping northward for the purpose of capturing Culpeper. The two armies met in a little valley about five miles southwest of the Hudson House. Standing on the porch of his headquarters, Pope could see the scene as pictured below. The haze of battle already hung over it. To his ears came the rumble of the guns as they roared death into the ranks of struggling men.

The mountain that rises above the valley was known as Cedar Mountain and upon its summit was the home of a man named Slaughter. People sometimes called the mountain, "Slaughter's Mountain",—a name strangely fitting after the dreadful battle fought upon its slopes in which thousands of brave men died on both sides without accomplishing any result of military value.

58

SLAUGHTER'S HOUSE ON THE SUMMIT OF CEDAR MOUNTAIN

THE STORM OF BATTLE HAS JUST PASSED

A FEW SURVIVORS OF A CHARGE THAT LEFT HUNDREDS DEAD UPON THE FIELD

THE SACRIFICE THAT EVERY WAR DEMANDS

CHAPTER SEVEN

The Second Battle of Bull Run

For two days the exhausted armies faced each other. Neither dared to make the first move. Then both quietly withdrew. For three weeks, General Lee and General Pope sparred for some advantage, then, like a thunderbolt out of the sky, the daring Southern cavalry leader, J. E. B. Stuart, in a torrential storm of rain and in the darkness of the night of August 22, hurled his forces against Catlett's Station, where Pope had established headquarters. The guards were quickly over-powered. Quantities of supplies, as well as Pope's secret papers, were carried off. The enemy had struck directly at the rear of the Federal lines.

NEAR THIS HOUSE THE CONFEDERATE GENERAL WINDER WAS KILLED BY A SHELL

NEGRO REFUGEES FLEEING NORTHWARD AS THE FEDERAL ARMY RETREATED

The loss of his supplies was a stunning blow for Pope. He began, at once, a retreat towards Washington. Lee, with a huge army, drawn from Richmond, followed, raiding and destroying wherever and whenever possible. Thus the two armies approached the historic spot on Bull Run, where the Federal forces, just a year before, had suffered such a disastrous defeat.

General Lee, meanwhile, completely outwitted General Pope. When he had convinced that officer that he intended to attack him, with all his forces, on the front, he quietly sent "Stonewall" Jackson up through the valley, west of the Bull Run Mountains. On the 26th of August, Jackson drove through Thoroughfare Gap and descended on the Federal supply base at Manassas Junction. Pope learned of the attack too late. Even as he hastened northward, Jackson's men were carrying off or destroying an enormous quantity of supplies.

On the two days that followed, Pope tried desperately to trap Jackson and destroy him, but that skilful commander evaded easily every effort of the Federal

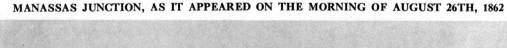

MANASSAS JUNCTION, AS IT APPEARED ON THE MORNING OF AUGUST 26TH, 1862

THE SECOND BATTLEFIELD OF BULL RUN, AUGUST, 1862

forces. In the meantime, the Southern division of General Longstreet's army arrived and turned the tide of battle. Once more, in the exact spot where disaster had overtaken them before, the Federal army was thrown into confusion and forced to retreat on the defences surrounding Washington.

This was not an easy matter. Railroads and bridges had been destroyed. Roads had been torn up to prevent the speedy passage of heavy artillery. Food supply wagon trains had been scattered or destroyed.

When the Federal soldiers crossed the little bridge, shown in the picture below, they not only put Bull Run between themselves and their pursuers, but they turned Pope's proud attempt to capture Richmond into a Confederate advance upon the city of Washington.

DESTROYED BY THE ARMY OF GENERAL LEE

READY TO ROLL AGAIN

AFTER A CONFEDERATE RAID, THIS IS THE SORT OF THING THAT CONFRONTED THE FEDERAL ENGINEERS.   IN A BRIEF SPACE OF TIME THIS ENGINE WAS RIGHTED AND REPAIRED AND SET GOING ONCE MORE

CONFEDERATE RAIDERS RIPPING UP THE RAILS OF A TRACK LEADING INTO WASHINGTON

COMPANY C OF THE FIGHTING FORTY-NINTH REGIMENT OF NEW YORK
THESE MEN PLAYED AN IMPORTANT PART IN THE SECOND BATTLE OF BULL RUN

BIVOUACED FOR THE NIGHT WITHIN A FEW MILES OF WASHINGTON

FAIRFAX COURT HOUSE PHOTOGRAPHED DURING THE RETREAT. NOTE THE MEN WATCHING THE ADVANCE OF THE CONFEDERATE FORCES FROM THE CUPOLA OF THE BUILDING!

Pope's flight from the field of Bull Run gave the Confederate cavalry leader a splendid chance to raid the retreating army. His object was to capture Fairfax Court House, a spot about twenty miles from the city of Washington. A vast amount of supplies had been collected in its vicinity which the Confederate army needed. On September 1st, Stuart tried to force his way down the pike leading to the Court House, but the Federal resistance proved too great and he was compelled to withdraw. The next day, however, General Pope was ordered to bring his men into Washington. As they departed, Stuart closed in and captured the Court House and a quantity of military stores which, a little later, proved most valuable, when General Lee moved north in his invasion of Maryland.

The student must have noted by this time how generalship, rather than the fighting qualities of the soldiers often determines the outcome of any battle. No braver men ever faced the fire of an enemy than the soldiers of the North and yet, in spite of heroism and sacrifice, these men were unable to hold their own against the superior strategy of such southern leaders as Johnston, Jackson and Lee. In war, as in peace, the mind is mightier than the sword.

Our chapter closes with two pictures of the bridges that spanned the Potomac in the vicinity of Washington. It is interesting to note that, in the lower bridge, the plank flooring has been removed in order to prevent a cavalry dash into the city of Washington, itself.

It must have been a source of great satisfaction for the people of the South to learn that, while McClellan lay for months within five miles of Richmond, Lee had literally pounded on the gates of Washington.

Once more the glow of Confederate campfires could be seen within fifteen miles of the Capital of the North.

ANTIETAM BRIDGE

This historic bridge spanned Antietam Creek. The photograph was taken soon after the battle. On the night of September 16th, 1862, the Federal cavalry captured this bridge and held it until the arrival of the infantry. During the battle, the fire of the artillery, posted near the bridge, saved the Federal forces from a disastrous repulse. This picture is very remarkable, as a photograph, because of its composition and tone value.

THE NINETY-THIRD NEW YORK INFANTRY JUST BEFORE THE BATTLE

CHAPTER EIGHT

ANTIETAM

General Lee was so pleased with his victory at the second battle of Bull Run that he decided to press northward in the hope of sweeping around the City of Washington by a bold dash through Maryland and Pennsylvania.

On the 3d of September, 1862, he crossed the Potomac near Leesburg, about thirty miles above the Federal Capital. His movements were not opposed and, on September 7th, he reached Frederick, where he tried to induce the people of Maryland to swing over to the Southern cause. Less than five hundred Marylanders responded to his appeal. Lee's invasion of the North caused great excitement in such cities as Baltimore and Philadelphia. The outcome of the two battles fought at Bull Run was not forgotten, and many people seriously feared that the invasion might mean the cutting off of Washington from the rest of the North.

Meanwhile, General McClellan, realizing fully the danger to the Federal Capital, had reorganized his army and set out in pursuit of his daring opponent. With one hundred thousand men, he reached Frederick on the 12th of September. Lee had, of course, moved northward. Apparently by accident, McClellan captured the Southern General's orders for the campaign. From these documents he learned that Lee had divided his army, sending a large number of men, under "Stonewall" Jackson and two other leaders, to take possession of Harper's Ferry.

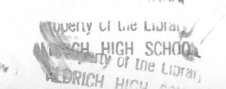

HARPER'S FERRY—NORTH BANK—JUST BEFORE JACKSON ARRIVED

Harper's Ferry, lying at the mouth of the Shenandoah River, was of great importance to Lee, since it not only provided him with a base for much needed supplies and reinforcements, but offered, also, a means of retreat, should the fortunes of war go against him. While "Stonewall" Jackson was swiftly moving south and west from Frederick to capture this important spot, Lee, himself, with the body of his troops, leisurely crossed South Mountain on his way towards Hagerstown.

McClellan understood well the importance of preventing the capture of Harper's Ferry. In and around the spot were stored huge quantities of supplies of all kinds. As soon as he learned of Lee's plans, he sent instructions at once to the Federal General in command to hold the town. Instead of moving at once to the assistance of his comrades, he delayed, as usual. The result of his delay was fatal to the Federal forces. Jackson arrived and set up his artillery on the hills around the Ferry. The Federal Commander, seeing only the slaughter of his men, if he resisted, sent up the white flag and surrendered. Twelve thousand, five hundred Federal soldiers were thus lost to the Northern cause,—as well as vast stores of military supplies.

McClellan now started once more in pursuit of Lee, hoping to bring him to battle before the Confederate armies around Harper's Ferry could move north to his aid.

When Lee found himself closely followed by a superior Federal force, he turned southward so as to keep his men in touch with the Potomac River. He knew, only too well, the importance of not being trapped on the northern bank. If he *had* to fight, he determined to open battle on a field of his own choosing.

Antietam Creek enters the Potomac River about seven miles above Harper's Ferry. Two and a half miles above the spot where the waters join, the Potomac

HARPER'S FERRY—SOUTH BANK—AFTER ITS EVACUATION BY GENERAL LEE

makes a sharp eastern bend that brings it back to within two and a half miles of Antietam Creek. At the center of this peninsula lay Sharpsburg, an ideal spot for any army to defend. The Shepherdstown Ford, an easy path across the Potomac, lay in the rear of the Confederate lines. Once more, Lee, one of the ablest generals of all time, had set the stage either for victory or defeat. In the picture below, we have a beautiful glimpse of the little village as it appeared on that eventful 17th of September, 1862.

SHARPSBURG ON THE MORNING OF THE BATTLE

**THIS LITTLE RED BRICK CHURCH LAY A MILE NORTH OF SHARPSBURG
AROUND IT THE BATTLE RAGED IN THE EARLY MORNING HOURS**

Antietam Creek was not much of an obstacle to a determined army. It was easily fordable in several places and was spanned by three stone bridges. Beyond it, however, the Confederates had thrown up entrenchments, and behind these barriers crouched a body of trained veterans whose courage had been tested in many battles. One part of the Federal Army crossed the little stream in the night, while two other sections, under Generals Burnside and Sumner, remained on the eastern bank. General Hooker, commanding the force that had crossed in the night, at dawn, moved down from the north and attacked in the vicinity of the little church shown above. In the picture below, we see the actual battlefield over which the two forces struggled in what has been called the bloodiest battle of the whole war. One side would have the advantage, only to be swept back by a terrific rush of new troops called up by the other. Soon the field was covered with dead and wounded men,—the soldiers of both sides,—lying in tangled masses, so close together that it was impossible, without close examination, to tell them apart. Some idea of the fury of the battle may be gained by studying the way in which the rail fences have been torn down and scattered about the field. Two thousand men fell in this spot in the early hours of that fateful day.

Not far from the little church was a sunken road, known to history as "Bloody Lane." The Confederate soldiers had turned this sunken road into a fortress by cutting down trees, and building barricades of their trunks and such rail fences

ON THIS FIELD TWO THOUSAND MEN FELL WITHIN THE SPACE OF A FEW HOURS

'HERE "STONEWALL" JACKSON'S MEN TRIED HARD TO STOP THE FEROCIOUS CHARGE OF HOOKER'S SOLDIERS

as were to be found in the neighborhood. Before capturing this spot, the Federal soldiers lost nearly a third of their total. One regiment lost sixty percent of the men who were sent against it. Bravery, such as was shown on both sides in this terrible battle, has seldom been seen in the history of the world. Men advanced without faltering, on both sides, knowing, from what they had already seen, that their next step would probably be their last.

A glance into the dreadful trench, shown in the pictures on page 74, will prove that *here* was a battle in which men did not retreat,—preferring rather to stay, even if they stayed in death.

The Federal forces were finally victorious,—about 1 o'clock in the afternoon,—and occupied the sunken road. Then began an artillery duel that lasted for most of the remaining hours of daylight.

Meanwhile, fresh reinforcements had arrived for the Federal side and the Commanding General, Franklin, urged, with all his strength, that a great assault be made upon the center of the Confederate lines. He argued that these men were worn out with the day's fighting and weakened with their losses and could be be easily driven back. If this could be accomplished, the line of retreat across the Potomac, by way of the Shepherdstown Ford, would be cut off, and Lee's whole army would be placed in danger. Again, with that strange way he had of giving Lee time to escape, McClellan vetoed the plan. Historians have said, in his defence, that he greatly overestimated the number of men that Lee had in reserve, and that the stubborn defence which the Southern soldiers had made, had impressed him to such an extent that he doubted his ability to overcome them. In any case, with the capture of the sunken road, the battle practically came to and end. Lee had not been defeated. The armies faced each other the following day. No battle was fought. That night, Lee slipped silently across the Potomac and retreated toward Winchester, Virginia.

IN THIS OLD SUNKEN ROAD LIES THE MUTE EVIDENCE OF THE STUBBORNESS
AND BRAVERY WITH WHICH THE CONFEDERATES FOUGHT

"BLOODY LANE," OVER WHICH THE BATTLE SURGED IN THE MOST TERRIBLE STRUGGLE
OF THE ENTIRE DAY

BURNSIDE BRIDGE—SO NAMED, AFTER THE STRUGGLE, TO COMMEMORATE THE SPOT WHERE THE BATTLE MIGHT HAVE BEEN WON

When the battle opened, Burnside had been left on the eastern bank of Antietam Creek. He had been told to hold himself in readiness to cross the bridge, shown above, and attack the Confederate forces that were entrenched along the heights that flanked the stream. About seven o'clock he was ordered to prepare to advance. Opposing him, was only a light body of infantry. At his back was one of the best divisions of the Federal Army. General McClellan testified afterwards that he sent Burnside the order to advance at about *eight* o'clock. Burnside said that such an order did not reach him until *ten*. Even if this be true, he did not move forward until *one* o'clock. Then followed another delay of *two hours*.

It was nearly *four* o'clock, three hours after the battle for the sunken road had been decided, that he finally made an assault upon the bridge shown in the picture above. After two serious blunders, in which one of his commanders missed a ford he had been sent to take and another missed the very bridge, itself, Burnside started to move his men towards Sharpsburg. Had this bridge been crossed, early in the day, as planned, the entire Confederate force would have been outflanked and decisively defeated. To make matters worse, a fresh body of Confederate troops came up from Harper's Ferry, before Burnside could get more than half of his men into action. The Federal forces were hurled back with heavy losses and sent flying in wild disorder across the very bridge they had just carried. In this needless and wholly useless operation, Burnside lost two thousand, two hundred, ninety three, killed, wounded and missing.

It was such wastage of young lives that saddened the hearts of the people of both North and South.

75

AN ACTUAL PICTURE OF THE BATTLE FOG THAT OVERSPREAD THE FIELD AT ANTIETAM

THIS LUTHERN CHURCH ON MAIN STREET, TO THE EAST OF SHARPSBURG, MARKED THE END OF THE FEDERAL ADVANCE. BEYOND THE VILLAGE, THE ROAD SHOWN IN THE PICTURE BECOMES THE SHEPHERDSTOWN PIKE LEADING DOWN TO THE FORD THAT LEE USED IN HIS RETREAT AFTER THE BATTLE

76

UNDER SUCH FLIMSY SHELTERS AS THESE THE WOUNDED LAY FOR HOURS

In the picture above we see one of the horrible sides of war not commonly understood by people who have not experienced war, itself. The number of wounded was so great in this one day's battle that the houses in the neighborhood were soon filled to overflowing, and men had to be cared for in the most primitive way. In this picture we see low tents,—mere shelters from the sun,—held aloft by means of musket barrels and bayonets. From Smith's barn, shown in the picture below, hay was hastily dragged, to be used as bedding for the torn bodies of the soldiers who were being constantly brought in from the fields. Dr. A. Hurd, a surgeon of the Fourteenth Indiana Volunteers, may be seen standing among the tents. The services of such men as Dr. Hurd became so highly respected on both sides that, on June 6th, 1862, an order was issued from Washington that surgeons should no longer be treated as prisoners of war and sent to prison. The order followed a similar order, *issued ten days before, by "Stonewall" Jackson.*

A BARN THAT WAS TURNED INTO A HOSPITAL

77

PRESIDENT LINCOLN VISITS THE CAMP AFTER THE BATTLE OF ANTIETAM. IT WAS HERE
HE MADE UP HIS MIND TO FREE THE SLAVES.

TWO WEEKS LATER, PRESIDENT LINCOLN VISITED CAMP AGAIN. HE IS HERE SHOWN TALKING WITH McCLELLAN. SHORTLY AFTER THIS VISIT, McCLELLAN WAS RELIEVED OF HIS COMMAND.

While the result of the Battle of Antietam was not decisive, it lifted a great fear from the hearts of the people of the North. It had, at least, removed the danger of invasion. Lee was retreating. Washington, for the time being, at least, was safe. While the President was deeply concerned because McClellan did not take up the pursuit of Lee at once, he was, nevertheless, emboldened to issue his Provisional Proclamation of Emancipation, in which he notified the South that, if, on the 1st of the following January, resistance should still continue, he would *free the slaves* and receive such as should desire to enlist into the armed service of the United States.

IN THIS PICTURE AND ITS CONTINUATION ON THE NEXT PAGE, WE SEE THE LITTLE TOWN OF BERLIN, MARYLAND, JUST AS IT LOOKED THE DAY GENERAL McCLELLAN STARTED IN PURSUIT OF LEE

A VIEW OF A TYPICAL CAMP SCENE, WHENEVER THE SOLDIERS RESTED IN ONE SPOT FOR SOME TIME. NOTICE THE BARRELS PLACED ON THE STOVES TO INCREASE THE DRAFT

BERLIN, MARYLAND, WHERE McCLELLAN RESTED UNTIL ORDERED BY PRESIDENT LINCOLN
TO TAKE UP THE PURSUIT OF THE DEFEATED CONFEDERATE ARMY

CHAPTER NINE

Fredericksburg

After his defeat at Antietam, General Lee crossed the Potomac and fell back upon the village of Winchester. President Lincoln insisted that the pursuit of Lee be taken up at once, but McClellan, as usual, made one excuse after another until, on the 6th of October, the President took matters into his own hands and ordered the pursuit to begin. McClellan did not obey. It was not until November that he crossed the Potomac on the bridge shown in the picture on page 80, and began a southern march, moving his troops down along the *eastern* side of the Blue Ridge Mountains.

Meanwhile, Lee had broken camp at Winchester and was moving south also, only he routed his march along the *western* side of the same mountains. The two armies came together at Culpeper. Before any battle could begin, President Lincoln, his patience at last exhausted, removed McClellan from his command and handed the direction of the army over to General Burnside.

Burnside immediately determined to move his whole force southward in an attack on Fredericksburg, since at that village he would have the advantage of reinforcements and supplies through Aquia Landing, a spot on the Potomac River connected with Fredericksburg by a railroad.

As Burnside moved south on the north side of the Rappahannock River, Lee accompanied him, step by step, on the other bank. Lee was taking no chances. At all costs he was determined to prevent his antagonist from making a dash for Richmond through a flanking movement.

A PIER MADE OF PONTOONS AT AQUIA CREEK LANDING ON THE POTOMAC RIVER

THESE SOLDIERS HAVE JUST DISEMBARKED FROM THE TRANSPORT AT THE LANDING

PLACING THE BREAD DOUGH IN THE PORTABLE OVEN. ARMY BREAD WAS EXCELLENT

In preparation for his attack on Fredericksburg, the little landing on Aquia Creek became, almost overnight, the busiest spot on the Potomac. Transports slid in and docked and discharged troops and supplies. These were hurriedly transferred to the north shore of the Rappahannock opposite Fredericksburg. Lee made no effort to hinder these operations. He believed in letting the enemy waste his strength in attacks on strong entrenchments. Very carefully, he posted eighty thousand men along the heights in the rear of the village.

In order to appreciate the difficulties involved in moving large bodies of men from place to place, it is well, at this time, to present a few of the wonderful scenes that the photographers of the Civil War have left us. Below are scenes that deal with the feeding of the army. In order to fight well, men must be fed well. In the Federal Army, vast sums were spent in the effort to keep the fighting spirit of the men at a high level. The situation was different in the South, due, not to any neglect on the part of the authorities, but to the scarcity of food and clothing that resulted from the close blockade of the Confederate ports by the ships of the navy.

Your attention is called to the picture, "Watering the Horses", on page 84.

EVERY LOAF HAD TO BE WEIGHED AND RECORDED

READY TO GO INTO ACTION AT A MOMENT'S NOTICE. SOLDIERS RODE THE HORSES THAT PULLED THE GUNS IN ORDER TO BE ABLE TO GUIDE THEM INSTANTLY INTO POSITION FOR BATTLE

When we understand that photography was a new art at the time this picture was taken, eighty years ago, we cannot help being astonished at its beauty. Another remarkable picture will be found on page 99.

WATERING THE HORSES. IT IS EVENING IN CAMP. THERE IS NO HINT OF THE SAVAGERY OF WAR IN THIS PEACEFUL SCENE

A FEDERAL BATTERY CAUGHT AT THE MOMENT THE GUNS ARE BEING FIRED

On the 17th of October, the Federal Army reached Falmouth, a little town on the north bank of the Rappahannock, opposite Fredericksburg. The bridges had been destroyed. Lee had no intention of trying to keep Burnside from crossing the river. He preferred to permit the crossing and fight the battle along the high ridges which he had fortified in the rear of the town.

In order to clear the opposing shore of sharpshooters, whose deadly accuracy took a terrible toll of life among the engineers working to span the river with pontoon bridges, batteries, similar to the one shown above, hurled tons of shells into the houses that lined the river's edge. In this picture, the guns are actually being fired and the slight haze that obscures the scene is the result of powder smoke.

General Burnside had accepted the post of Commander of the Army of the Potomac with great reluctance. He insisted that he was not the man for the job. The President thought otherwise. When Burnside arrived before Fredericksburg, he called a meeting of all his subordinate Generals. He was in favor of crossing the river and taking the heights beyond by storm. The other Generals shook their heads. They pointed out, one after the other, the facts that had to be faced. Lee had entrenched his men on Marye's Heights. He had plenty of big guns to support his infantry. His men were behind stone walls with plenty of ammunition. In spite of all this advice, Burnside decided to make the attack.

From his headquarters in the Phillips House, he directed, personally, the disastrous assault that wrote December 13th, 1862, into the history of the United States as one of its bloodiest memories.

At nightfall of that fatal day, General Sumner's men retired from the attack, leaving five thousand four hundred men dead or wounded on the slopes of Marye's Heights. "Oh, those men, those men over there!" cried Burnside, "I cannot get them out of my mind!"

85

THE PHILLIPS HOUSE, FROM WHICH BURNSIDE DIRECTED THE FATAL BATTLE OF
DECEMBER 13TH, 1862

THE LACEY HOUSE WHICH GENERAL SUMNER USED AS HIS HEADQUARTERS DURING THE
BATTLE

FEDERAL SIGNAL OFFICERS STUDYING THE POSITIONS OF LEE ACROSS THE RAPPAHANNOCK

FREDERICKSBURG, JUST BEFORE THE PONTOON BRIDGES WERE LAID FOR THE ASSAULT

In this remarkable picture, the photographer has preserved for us a view of the village as it appeared just before the soldiers crossed to the attack. The old mill, a close-up of which is to be seen on page 95, escaped damage, although its windows were lined with sharpshooters. Along the hills in the far distance, the army of Lee lay waiting behind its entrenchments. In the lower picture, by following Telegraph Road, we come to Marye's Heights, a place of death and suffering for thousands of Federal soldiers. Along this road the Federal Army advanced that terrible morning. Shells falling on them from the batteries beyond the town, thinned their ranks every foot of the way. They had been ordered to march and, although their own commanders considered the order unwise, march they did without faltering to their doom.

TELEGRAPH ROAD, LEADING UP FROM THE RIVER TO MARYE'S HEIGHTS

ONLY THE PIERS MARK THE SPOT WHERE A BEAUTIFUL BRIDGE HAD STOOD A
SHORT WHILE BEFORE

This photograph was taken from the north side of the river and shows the very trenches used by the Federal troops just before they began the ill-fated crossing of the river. The trenches in the foreground were full of troops dressed neatly in new, blue uniforms. From the higher ground, on the right, Federal batteries shelled the town across the river.

Shortly after three o'clock of the morning of the 11th of December, long columns of soldiers moved down to the water's edge and, before daybreak, hidden for some time by a dense fog, the pontoniers began laying the bridges made of boats. Confederate sharpshooters were busy. They drove off the men laying two of the bridges, and their fire was so accurate and deadly that Sumner decided to save lives by driving them off. As the mist cleared, he sent soldiers across in boats. These men landed and scattered through the houses along the water's edge. The fire of the sharpshooters faded away. At daybreak, the bridges were completed and the troops began to cross. It took all of that day to get the main body of the army into Fredericksburg. Late in the morning of the 13th, confused orders began to

A PONTOON ON THE WAGON THAT CARRIED IT FROM STREAM TO STREAM

DOWN STREETS LINED WITH WRECKED HOMES THE SOLDIERS OF THE NORTH TRAMPED TO THEIR DEATH

---

arrive from Burnside who had remained on the other side of the river. Sumner was to go forward and capture Marye's Heights. Then began the dreadful march down Telegraph Road.

An interesting story is told about the bridge on the left of the picture. The men were ordered to cross swiftly and they broke into a double-quick step. They had been so well drilled and the drums to which they marched kept up such a steady beat that the bridge soon began to vibrate. The vibration became so violent that it threatened to break the boats apart. One of the Federal leaders, noticing the danger, spurred his horse through the ranks of the men, shouting as he plunged forward for them to break step. In order to avoid the horse, the soldiers had to dive into the water. By quick thinking and quick acting, the bridge was saved.

THESE PONTOONS WERE LAID IN THE EARLY MORNING UNDER COVER OF A FOG

89

THIS BATTERY PROTECTED THE SOLDIERS AS THEY RUSHED FORWARD TO THE ATTACK

THE TERRIBLE RESULTS OF ONE OF THE SHELLS FIRED BY THE BATTERY SHOWN ABOVE

HIT BY A SHELL FROM A FEDERAL CANNON

BEHIND THE CONFEDERATE LINES ON MARYE'S HEIGHTS

MARYE'S HEIGHTS, BEFORE WHOSE DOORS THOUSANDS OF SOLDIERS DIED. NOTICE THE TRENCH ON THE LEFT OF THE PICTURE! FROM THIS, THE CONFEDERATES POURED A WITHERING FIRE INTO THE ADVANCING LINES

"Marye's House marked the center of the Confederate position on the Heights, before which the Federals fell three deep in one of the bravest and bloodiest assaults of the war. The eastern boundary of the Marye estate was a retaining wall, along which ran a sunken road; on the other side of this was a stone wall, shoulder high, forming a perfect infantry parapet. Here two brigades of Confederates were posted and on the crest above them were the supporting batteries, while the slope between was honeycombed with the rifle-pits of the sharpshooters, one of which is seen in the picture. Six times did the Federals, raked by the deadly fire of the Washington Artillery, advance to within a hundred yards of the sunken road, only to be driven back by the rapid volleys of the Confederate infantry concealed there. Less than three of every five men in Hancock's division came back from their charge on these death-dealing heights. The complete repulse of the day and the terrific slaughter were the barren results of an heroic effort to obey orders."—Eggleston.

SOLDIERS LAY FIVE DEEP, IN PLACES, IN THIS SUNKEN ROAD

WOUNDED INDIAN SHARPSHOOTERS BEING GIVEN FIRST AID ON THE FIELD OF BATTLE

93

WAITING TO BE TAKEN TO A HOSPITAL IN SOME PRIVATE HOME. THESE MEN ARE INDIANS.
THE PICTURE WAS TAKEN DURING THE SECOND BATTLE OF MARYE'S HEIGHTS WHEN
THOUSANDS DIED, STORMING ITS DEFENCES

CONFEDERATE ENTRENCHMENTS BEHIND THE LINES OF MARYE'S HEIGHTS

THE OLD MILL WHERE SOLDIERS OF THE NORTH AND THE SOUTH WERE GROUPED FOR A PHOTOGRAPH

So great had been the havoc on both sides during the battle of Fredericksburg that a truce was declared during which the blue and the gray mingled freely in the search for suffering comrades. Above, we have a truly wonderful picture, perhaps the only one in existence, showing soldiers of the South and the North posing for a photograph! This old mill may be seen in the picture on page 87.

Little is said about the part the Indian played in the Civil War, but here is evidence that the Redman fought on both sides with his white brothers. These men served the North as sharpshooters. Captain Ely S. Parker, one of Grant's favorite aides, was an Indian. He was appointed later to the rank of Colonel and it was he, who drafted, in beautiful penmanship, the terms of Lee's Surrender at Appomattox.

After the first day's battle had ceased, Burnside once more called his Generals into conference. He was in favor of another assault, but opposition to this plan was so great that he, at last, gave in. Thus ended the Battle of Fredericksburg. Once more the South had won.

WHILE GENERAL SICKLES OF THE FEDERAL ARMY IS REVIEWING THESE TROOPS (See next page) NUMBERING 18,000 MEN

HERE WAS FOUGHT THE MOST TERRIFIC ACTION IN THE BATTLE OF CHANCELLORSVILLE

"STONEWALL" JACKSON, WITH 31,000, IS SWEEPING SWIFTLY TO ATTACK THEM FROM THE REAR

CHAPTER TEN

CHANCELLORSVILLE

The Battle of Chancellorsville was really the continuation of the Battle of Fredericksburg, with a four month and a half intermission, in which the Federal forces lay on their arms on the north bank of the Rappahannock while the Confederates established themselves in winter quarters on the heights behind the village. Only the river separated the two great hosts. In the spring, by mutual consent, the men on both sides bathed in the stream. Toy boats were rigged up with sails and shuttled back and forth. The boats from the Confederate side would carry tobacco, while the return boat would have a cargo consisting of some northern article scarce in the south.

WHERE "STONEWALL" JACKSON FELL

FOR THE SECOND TIME THIS BATTERY HURLS ITS SHELLS INTO THE CONFEDERATE

The last of April came. Hooker was ready to strike. In order to deceive Lee, he, secretly, sent the main body of his army to Chancellorsville, ten miles west of Fredericksburg and two miles south of the Rappahannock River. In front of Fredericksburg, he left only enough men to make a convincing display.

Lee was not deceived. By a rapid night march, he met the Federal Army before it had reached the positions assigned to it. A battle followed, in which neither side had the advantage. On May 2nd, the real struggle began. Night came, but the firing continued. General "Stonewall" Jackson, with his staff, rode out into the darkness to try to locate the Federal forces. Through a fatal blunder, his own men fired upon him, inflicting a fatal wound. The Battle of Chancellorsville ended the following day. With the memory of Jackson spurring them on, the men of the South drove the Federals before them, but there was sorrow in their hearts. They had lost one of their ablest Generals, a soldier, who, second only to Lee, had proven more than a match for the leaders the North had sent against him.

ENTRENCHMENTS LOCATED ON THE DEADLY SLOPES OF MARYE'S HEIGHTS

In order to try to trap Lee, the army before Fredericksburg crossed the river and attacked Marye's Heights. This time the trenches were carried but only after thousands of dead had once more heaped the sunken road to its very brim. The sacrifice was all in vain. Lee's victorious forces returned to Fredericksburg and drove the Federal forces to the river's edge. That night they escaped across the Rappahannock. Thousands had died on both sides. Once more the South had won its victory. The people of the North grieved over their dead. The people of the South wept bitter tears, also,—for "Stonewall" Jackson lay critically ill near Chancellorsville.

In the pictures on the next page we have two splendid views of the battlefield taken shortly after the conflict. General Howard, one of the Federal Commanders, had encamped in the open space around the church. His men had stacked their arms and were preparing for the night. Suddenly, herds of deer sdarted acros the clearing. This was the first intimation Howard had that a large body of men was approaching. Needless to say, the Confederates, under "Stonewall" Jackson, scattered the Federal forces in all directions.

WILDERNESS CHURCH, ABOUT WHICH RAGED A TERRIFIC BATTLE WHEN JACKSON'S
WARRIORS SURPRISED THE FEDERAL SOLDIERS AS THEY WERE COOKING SUPPER

ACROSS THIS SPOT SWEPT THE FAMOUS CHARGE OF THE EIGHTH PENNSYLVANIA CAVALRY

A SUPPLY BASE FOR THE FEDERAL ARMY AT BELLE PLAIN

A QUIET EVENING IN CAMP

PEOPLE GATHERING AT GETTYSBURG TO HEAR THE FOLLOWING IMMORTAL WORDS:

"Fourscore and seven years ago our fathers brought forth on this continent a new nation, conceived in liberty, and dedicated to the proposition that all men are created equal. Now we are engaged in a great civil war, testing whether that nation, or any nation so conceived and so dedicated, can long endure. We are met on a great battlefield of that war. We have come to dedicate a portion of that field as a final resting-place for those who here gave their lives that that nation might live. It is altogether fitting and proper that we should do this. But in a larger sense, we cannot dedicate, we cannot consecrate, we cannot hallow this ground. The brave men, living and dead, who struggled here, have consecrated it far above our poor power to add or detract. The world will little note, nor long remember, what we say here, but it can never forget what they did here. It is for us, the living, rather, to be dedicated here to the unfinished work which they who fought here have thus far so nobly advanced. It is rather for us to be here dedicated to the great task remaining before us;—that from these honored dead, we take increased devotion to that cause for which they gave the last full measure of devotion;—that we here highly resolve that these dead shall not have died in vain, that this nation, under God, shall have a new birth of freedom, and that government of the people, by the people, for the people, shall not perish from the earth."

IN THE DISTANCE, WHILE THIS PICTURE WAS BEING TAKEN, PRESIDENT LINCOLN
WAS DELIVERING HIS GETTYSBURG ADDRESS

CHAPTER ELEVEN

GETTYSBURG

With the defeat of Hooker's army at Chancellorsville, the demand for an invasion of the North grew rapidly in the South. People pointed to Bull Run and Cedar Mountain and Fredericksburg as proof that the Southern armies were a match for those of the North on any field. Food was becoming scarce, and ammunition was not as plentiful as the leaders wished. If the North could be invaded and Washington captured, many believed that the war would come to an end,—if not in a direct victory for the South, at least in a compromise that would leave things as they were before the first gun had been fired.

Under the spur of this urging, Lee moved towards the North once more. He left General Stuart, with ten thousand cavalry to prevent General Hooker from following in his rear. Lee had, at this time, a force of one hundred thousand men. With this huge army behind him, he began his march down the Shenandoah Valley early in June. He carefully kept the Blue Ridge Mountains between his men and the Federal forces.

Hooker, disregarding the movements of Stuart's cavalry, followed his opponent. He went north along the *eastern* side of the same mountains. After several attempts to induce Hooker to cross over for an attack, Lee concentrated his entire force at Winchester. He captured this important little village by surprise and took two thousand prisoners.

On the 24th and 25th of June, the Confederate Army crossed the Potomac at two places,—almost within sight of the battle-field of Antietam. The two columns came together at Hagerstown, Maryland, and then pressed on towards the Pennsylvania line.

THE LITTLE TOWN OF CULPEPER, VIRGINIA, WHERE LEE ASSEMBLED HIS FORCES

FEDERAL CAVALRY NEAR FREDERICKSBURG,—TRYING TO LOCATE
THE CONFEDERATE ARMY

On the 26th of June, Hooker also crossed the river, moving towards Frederick. On the very next day, Hooker resigned his command, and President Lincoln ordered General Meade to lead the troops. Lee had great respect for Meade and he came to the conclusion that it would be dangerous for him to march northward

AMMUNITION SUPPLY TRAINS ON THE WAY NORTH WITH HOOKER'S ARMY

GETTYSBURG, AS THE CONFEDERATE SOLDIERS SAW IT ON THE DAY OF BATTLE

---

any further without disposing of the army that threatened his right flank. He was in enemy country and could not count on the goodwill of the inhabitants. What supplies he could get, he had to take by force and this meant scattering thousands of his soldiers over the countryside. In the meanwhile, both great armies were moving slowly northward along parallel lines. General Meade never lost sight of the need of protecting the Capital. Wherever Lee went, he found a large Federal Army between him and the city of Washington.

Now it happened that there was a large supply of shoes in Gettysburg. Lee needed these shoes for his men and had sent an officer named Hess to seize them. Riding in from the opposite side, came Major Kress of the Federal force, who had been sent by General Wadsworth on the same errand. In the town, itself, was General Buford, Commander of two brigades of Federal cavalry. Two miles north-east of Gettysburg, the two advance columns collided. This was the beginning of the great battle which neither Lee nor Meade had planned for this particular spot. When the cry for reinforcements reached headquarters on both sides, it became certain that a decisive battle was about to open.

(*Narrative is continued on page* 112)

TROOPS DRAWN UP IN A "HOLLOW SQUARE" TO MEET A RUSH OF CAVALRY

McPHERSON'S WOODS, WHERE GENERAL REYNOLDS FELL DURING THE BATTLE
THAT DELAYED THE ADVANCE OF THE CONFEDERATE FORCES

GENERAL WARREN LEFT THESE MEN BEHIND AS HE SWEPT UPWARD ALONG THE SLOPES OF
LITTLE ROUND TOP. AN HOUR LOST AT THIS SPOT MIGHT HAVE PROVED THE
TURNING POINT IN THE BATTLE THAT FOLLOWED

"THE SLAUGHTER PEN" . . . BETWEEN THE ROUND TOPS. AT THIS RAVINE THE
CONFEDERATE FORCES MADE A DETERMINED EFFORT TO BREAK THROUGH
THE FEDERAL LINES

THE HEIGHTS FOR WHICH SOLDIERS ON BOTH SIDES LAID DOWN THEIR LIVES

TREES BLASTED BY THE ARTILLERY FIRE THAT SWEPT THIS HILL

LITTLE ROUND TOP . . . DURING THE SECOND DAY'S BATTLE THIS SPOT WAS NEARLY LOST TO THE FEDERAL CAUSE. GENERAL WARREN SAVED THE DAY

NEAR THE SUMMIT OF LITTLE ROUND TOP WAS A CHASM KNOWN AS "THE DEVIL'S DEN". AFTER ITS CAPTURE, ON THE SECOND DAY, IT WAS USED AS A POST FOR CONFEDERATE SHARPSHOOTERS

THE FIRST DAY'S TOLL. THESE MEN HELD UP THE CONFEDERATE ADVANCE, GIVING MEADE TIME TO BRING HIS FORCES TOGETHER

LITTLE ROUND TOP

ROWS OF DEAD, NOT FAR FROM THE PEACH ORCHARD ON TROSTLE'S FARM

THE "IRON BRIGADE" . . . THE TWENTY FOURTH MICHIGAN INFANTRY LEFT SEVEN
DISTINCT ROWS OF DEAD BEHIND IT AS IT FELL BACK FROM BATTLE LINE TO
BATTLE LINE DURING THE HEAVY FIGHTING ON THE FIRST DAY

AFTER THE BATTLE . . . NOT FAR FROM TROSTLE'S FARM

TROSTLE'S FARMYARD . . . AT THIS VERY SPOT BIGELOW'S NINTH MASSACHUSETTS BATTERY MADE ITS GLORIOUS STAND, CHECKING THE ADVANCING WAVES OF CONFEDERATE INFANTRY AS THEY RUSHED TOWARDS ROUND TOP HILL

General Reynolds, in command of the advance divisions of the Federal Army, stood his ground along a little creek at the edge of a thick woods. It was his intention to hold up the advance of the Confederates until Meade could bring forward his reinforcements. General Reynolds was killed early in the action.

A little after noon of July 2nd, both armies were concentrated and ready for battle. Each occupied ridges which were separated from each other by a valley. The Federal troops were on Cemetery Ridge, directly south of Gettysburg. The Confederate forces occupied Seminary Ridge.

Cemetery Ridge is about three miles long and is shaped like a fish-hook. On the extreme south, is *Round Top*. Next comes *Little Round Top*, which figures so prominently in the pictures that follow. Next to Little Round Top is *Cemetery Hill*.

Against these three hills the Confederate Army launched its most savage attacks. At three o'clock that afternoon, the Southern Commander, Longstreet, struck a heavy blow at the forces on Little Round Top. The summit had been left unguarded by the Federal forces, but an engineer, named Warren, saw the danger and rushed forward a few regiments to defend it. These men arrived just a few moments before the Confederates. The battle that followed raged all the afternoon around the Federal positions. The losses on both sides were very heavy. Ten thousand Federal soldiers lay on the field when darkness put an end to the battle.

TROSTLE'S HOUSE . . . GENERAL SICKLES, LEADER OF A FEDERAL DIVISION, MADE THIS OLD FARMHOUSE HIS HEADQUARTERS. THE DEAD HORSES BELONGED TO THE FEDERAL BATTERY THAT HAD BEEN ASSIGNED THE TASK OF DEFENDING THE SPOT

The next morning was spent by both sides in making preparations for the decisive battle that all knew was at hand. An hour after noon, the Confederate artillery began a heavy bombardment of the Ridge. This continued for two hours, during which the Federal artillery blasted the Confederate forces with heavy shells. In order that he might gauge the strength of the enemy guns, Meade, about this time, ordered his batteries to cease firing. Lee, noticing the absence of gun fire, was completely deceived. He thought that the Federal guns had been put out of action and that the infantry had become confused and frightened by his own bombardment. He, at once, ordered the grand attack to be made. Lee was deceived, also, as to the number of men opposing him. He had no idea that forty thousand trained soldiers held the opposite ridge.

A study of the pictures on these two pages will give one a vivid understanding of the terrible nature of the struggle that began with Lee's order. In this yard was stationed one of the Federal batteries. It was really an advance post set up to guard General Sickles's headquarters from surprise attacks. The Confederate advance, in its movement across the valley, rolled over this spot, engulfing horses and men. The wounded and dead soldiers had been removed, just before the pictures were taken, but the horses remain to tell their own grim story.

Not more than eighteen thousand men rushed forward at Lee's order. They consisted of Pickett's Virginians, supported by a number of brigades under the leadership of Pettigrew and Wilcox.

With a bravery seldom equalled in any part of the world, this picked division moved down the slope of Seminary Ridge and across the valley. They had hoped to have the support of the artillery posted on the heights behind them, but to Lee's dismay, he found that the terrific bombardment of the hours before had used up nearly all his ammunition. It was too late to bring up more. Pickett's men were on their way.

The advancing column showed a front of nearly a mile and thus became an enormous target for the Federal artillery, which now began to fire again. Shells tore great gaps in the advancing ranks but the steady march of the Southern soldiers did not falter. It was a terrifying sight to see this vast body of men moving with slow, but determined step, across the valley and towards the heights beyond.

It was Lee's intention to strike the Federal forces fairly in the center, cut them in two and roll back the edges. The men, waiting behind a low stone wall, were ordered to hold their fire until the Confederates were very close. This they did. When their guns finally blazed, the advancing ranks went down like grass before a

AN UNFINISHED GRAVE LEFT BEHIND BY THE CONFEDERATES AS THEY HASTILY RETREATED. A TORRENTIAL RAIN WAS FALLING AND THE GROUND WAS A MASS OF MUD

scythe. In spite of the withering fire, Pickett's men burst through the center and drove on until they found themselves fighting hand to hand amid the very guns of the Federal batteries. All was confusion. Instead of retreating, the Federal soldiers leaped in with clubbed guns and bayonets. For a dreadful half hour this battle roared along the crest of the Ridge, then, outnumbered, and weary from the struggle, the Virginians were driven back. Of that gallant band, not more than one in four escaped uninjured. The Confederate cause had lost sixteen thousand men.

During the night, a discouraged Lee brought all his forces together behind the barrier of Seminary Ridge. He expected Meade to attack at once and finish the work he had begun, but Meade hesitated. His losses had been very heavy and he was uncertain as to Lee's reserve strength. All that day he waited. Towards night a heavy storm burst over the countryside. Amid flashes of lightning and

WAITING FOR BURIAL

115

GENERAL MEADE'S HEADQUARTERS ON CEMETERY RIDGE

roaring thunder, Lee began his retreat. This was the 5th of July, 1863. By the 7th, he had reached the Potomac. He found it swollen by the heavy rains and not to be forded. The bridges had been destroyed. He was trapped on the north bank of the river,—a situation he had often feared, and against which he had often made preparations. While he hastily built a flimsy bridge, he entrenched his troops and waited for the attack he felt certain he must face.

Meade came within sight of the entrenchments on the 12th of the month. Once more he hesitated and once more, in the night, Lee vanished across the stream. The water had dropped a little and many of the Confederate soldiers were able to wade across, holding their equipment above their heads.

THE SURVIVORS OF THE BATTERY THAT HELPED CHECK PICKETT'S CHARGE

116

EMERGENCY HOSPITAL TENTS THAT SHELTERED THE WOUNDED AFTER THE BATTLE OF GETTYSBURG

The battle tide for the South had reached its highest point during the battle of Gettysburg. Not only *here*, but in the West, as we shall see in Book Two, the cause of the Confederacy had taken a downward turn. While the Federal victory was not decisive, the effect upon the people of the North was very great. There was hope now that the conflict would not go on forever. In the South, there was deep discouragement. Thoughtful persons began to understand that, under the pressure of the great manpower and resources of the North, there could be but one result of the struggle.

Once Lee had placed the Potomac between his army and the soldiers of the North, he marched south slowly as though certain that pursuit would not be pressed too hard. The same difficulties that faced him also faced Meade. It was necessary for the Federal General to swing through Harper's Ferry to get his men across the still swollen stream. By the time he had done so, Lee had placed his men in strong, entrenched positions along the south bank of the Rapidan River. Here he awaited whatever action Meade might take.

THE POTOMAC, BEYOND WHICH LAY SAFETY FOR LEE'S BATTERED TROOPS

MEADE'S ARMY LEISURELY CROSSING THE POTOMAC IN PURSUIT . . . EIGHTEEN DAYS
AFTER THE BATTLE OF GETTYSBURG

HOW THE RETREATING ARMY DESTROYED THE RAILROADS BEHIND IT

THE RAILROAD TIES WERE BURNED AND THE RAILS BENT AND WARPED WITH THE
HEAT . . . SOMETIMES, WHILE RED HOT, THE RAILS WERE WOUND AROUND TREES

A REMARKABLE PICTURE: . . . GENERAL GRANT, SITTING BEFORE THE LEFT HAND TREE IS ARRIVING AT HIS DECISION "TO FIGHT IT OUT ON THIS LINE IF IT TAKES ALL SUMMER" . . . THIS DECISION COST HIM TWO THOUSAND MEN THE FOLLOWING MORNING

120

IN THIS SPOT GENERAL GRANT TOOK COMMAND OF THE ARMY

CHAPTER TWELVE

THE WILDERNESS WITH GRANT IN COMMAND

All that winter the Confederate Army of Northern Virginia lay in winter quarters along the south bank of the Rapidan River. The position was naturally a strong one and had been reinforced with rifle-pits that commanded every ford. An assault in front was out of the question.

It was into a situation like this that Ulysses S. Grant was thrust, on the 19th of March, 1863, when Meade was removed and the warrior of the west placed in supreme command. Grant spent two months studying the problem.—Then, on the morning of May 4th, 1864, the Army of the Potomac marched, in two columns, for the lower fords of the Rapidan River. Since Grant had chosen a spot ten miles below Lee's entrenchments, the latter could do nothing to stop the passage of the troops. Perhaps the wise Southern leader did not *want* to stop them, for below, just a few hours' march away, lay the *Wilderness*,—a jungle of swamp and tangled vines and stunted trees. *Lee knew every inch of the country. Grant knew very little about it.* (*Narrative is continued on page* 124)

BELLE PLAIN LANDING ON THE POTOMAC WHERE SUPPLIES WERE ACCUMULATED

THE ARMY OF THE POTOMAC ADVANCES ACROSS THE RAPIDAN ON THE
MORNING OF MAY 5TH, 1864

FOUR MORE VIEWS OF BELLE PLAIN LANDING

THESE PONTOONS WERE LAID IN PLACE AT GERMANNA FORD

A CLOSER VIEW OF THE SAME SCENE THAT IS PICTURED ABOVE

A DISTANT VIEW OF THE RAPIDAN RIVER

When Grant entered the Wilderness, after crossing the Rapidan, he moved his men forward along two roads that cut through the swamp. Lee went to meet him along two other roads that cut Grant's path. Grant did not dream that Lee would select a place like the Wilderness for an attack, but that is just what Lee did. The troops came into conflict at the spot where the roads crossed and furious fighting raged until four o'clock in the afternoon.

THE WILDERNESS . . . A TYPICAL SCENE THAT SHOWS THE HARDSHIPS THAT FACED GRANT'S MEN

THE WRECKAGE OF TREES AND MEN . . . AFTER THE STORM OF BATTLE HAD PASSED

Neither side had any advantage and the battle was discontinued as though by mutual consent. The next morning, fighting was renewed and both sides were badly cut up, due to the broken ground over which they fought. In the late afternoon, a fire sprang up in the forest and a strong wind blew the smoke directly into the eyes of the Federal men. The Confederates attacked at once in the hope of surprising the Northern forces and overwhelming them. A desperate hand to hand struggle followed in which the Southern soldiers were driven back.

"BLOODY ANGLE" . . . A CONFEDERATE BARRICADE BEFORE WHICH HUNDREDS FELL ON BOTH SIDES

125

McCOOL'S HOUSE . . . AS IT APPEARED ON THE MORNING OF MAY 12TH, AS THE BATTLE
OF SPOTTSYLVANIA RAGED AROUND IT

During the two days of battle practically no artillery was used on either side.
The character of the country did not permit its use or easy transport. The soldiers
fought each other fiercely with bayonets and muskets, dodging for cover from tree
to tree as they surged back and forth across the area.

The next day, both sides were busy spying out the other's strength. On the
7th, Grant, believing that Lee was in no condition to attack him, moved his army
to the left, outflanking Lee and compelling him to abandon his strong entrenchments. In the evening of that day, the Federal Army moved towards Spottsylvania
Court House and Lee followed, reaching the vicinity of the Court House, itself,
ahead of Grant. The Southern soldiers at once threw up entrenchments and made
ready to resist an assault. The tactics of Grant, in always moving to the left and
thus outflanking his opponent, worried the Southern Generals. With every flanking
operation, Grant was drawing closer and closer to Richmond.

THE KIND OF COUNTRY THAT SLOWED DOWN THE MOVEMENTS OF GRANT'S ARMY

126

**AFTER THE BATTLE OF SPOTTSYLVANIA, SOLDIERS WERE BURIED WHERE THEY FELL
THIS BURIAL IS IN THE FARMYARD OF AN ABANDONED HOME**

While the results of the Battle of Spottsylvania did not seem to be decisive, since neither antagonist had been defeated, the fact that Grant continued his march southward encouraged the people of the North in the belief that, at last, they had discovered a General who knew how to advance *and keep on advancing*. Grant, also, understood the real meaning of the kind of battle he was waging for, in a communication to the War Department on the 11th, he wrote:

**THESE CONFEDERATE SOLDIERS BELONGED TO SOUTHERN GENERAL EWELL'S
CORPS. THEY AWAIT BURIAL BY THE VERY MEN WHOM THEY HAD FOUGHT
A FEW HOURS BEFORE**

THE WOUNDED, NORTH AND SOUTH ALIKE, WERE CARED FOR BY ARMY SURGEONS AFTER THE BATTLE

"We have now ended the sixth day of very hard fighting. The result to this day is very much in our favor. Our losses have been heavy, as well as those of the enemy. I propose to fight it out on this line if it takes all summer." His final success, however, was along a very different line and took not only all summer, but all autumn and all winter and part of another spring.

ON THE BACK OF THIS PICTURE WAS FOUND THE FOLLOWING: "ON THE BATTLEFIELD OF SPOTTSYLVANIA, IN THE REAR, DURING THE ACTION"

UNION ARTILLERY MASSING IN THE DISTANCE FOR THE ADVANCE. THE CONFEDERATE
ATTACK, HOWEVER, WAS SO SEVERE THAT THE ADVANCE WAS DELAYED . . .
THE TIME IS MAY 18, 1864

The terrible battle was not ended on the 12th of May. During the next five days
it raged with varying results. Each side was striving to find some weak spot through
which it could break in order to crumple up the other's flanks. At last, convinced
that it would be impossible to dislodge Lee from his entrenched positions, Grant,
instead of retreating, began to move around the Confederate right towards the
North Anna River. March was resumed on the 20th of May. The Federal soldiers
were so exhausted by the terrible days of struggle they had been through that many
fell asleep beside the way.

Upon the weary engineering corps, descended the full responsibility for the movements of the troops. These determined and brave men laid the pontoon bridges
and built the corduroy roads in the face of constant fire from sharpshooters.

OVER PONTOON BRIDGES SUCH AS THESE THE FEDERAL ARMY MADE ITS WAY
CAUTIOUSLY SOUTHWARD

129

THIS PICTURE AND ITS CONTINUATION ON PAGE 131 SHOW HOW PRISONERS WERE
HERDED INTO COMPACT MASSES IN ORDER THAT THEY MIGHT BE GUARDED
WITH A MINIMUM OF EFFORT AND CHANCE OF ESCAPE

IN THE PICTURE BELOW WE HAVE A SCENE OF IMMORTAL VALUE. IN SPITE OF THE FACT
THAT THE SNAPSHOT WAS UTTERLY UNKNOWN, THE PHOTOGRAPHER HAS CAPTURED FOR
US A FLEETING GLIMPSE OF GRANT AS HE CONFERRED WITH HIS MILITARY STAFF

AS THIS PICTURE WAS TAKEN, THE CONFEDERATE PRISONERS WERE ABOUT TO RECEIVE
THEIR RATIONS. THEY HAD JUST BEEN THROUGH A TERRIFIC PERIOD OF
BATTLE AND WERE EXHAUSTED AND HUNGRY

THIS IS A COMPANION PICTURE FOR THE ONE ON PAGE 130, IN WHICH GENERAL GRANT
IS SHOWN LEANING ON THE BACK OF THE SETTEE AT THE LEFT OF THE SCENE. IN THE
PICTURE IMMEDIATELY BELOW, HE IS SHOWN SITTING UNDER THE
TREE IN THE LEFT CENTER

QUARLES' MILL DAM: IT WAS IN THIS PLACE, WHERE HE HAD SET UP HEADQUARTERS, THAT GRANT DISCOVERED HIS MISTAKE IN PERMITTING HIS ARMY TO BE LED INTO A CLEVER TRAP SET BY LEE

The Federal Army had barely started towards the North Anna River when Lee detected the movement and, understanding its purpose, set to work to check its drive southward by a brilliant march of his own. As on the march from the Wilderness to Spottsylvania, Lee took the shorter way, along main highways, and thus was able to reach the North Anna River ahead of his antagonist. In the scene above, we have a view of one of the most vital spots in the entire southward march of the Federal forces. When the Northern Army reached the North Anna River, Warren, who commanded one flank, crossed without opposition. Lee was known to be on the south bank but he offered no resistance, much to the surprise of everyone. Warren crossed the river at Jericho Mills about a mile above the scene depicted above. Hancock, another of the Federal Generals, crossed over a wooden bridge just below the scene. This crossing was also unopposed.

Meanwhile, information had reached Grant that Lee had drawn back his two wings to form a great V, whose apex was just in front of his own quarters. He had deliberately permitted the right and left flanks of Grant's army to cross in order that he might march in between them, cut them off from each other and from Grant and then turn upon each, individually, and destroy it before it could be reunited to the main body.

This was the discovery that worried Grant, as he sat in one of the little white houses dimly seen on the hill. Unless he could find an immediate solution, the army of the North was faced with another disastrous defeat.

TWO PICTURES ON THIS PAGE SHOW THE PONTOON BRIDGE LAID FOR THE CROSSING OF GENERAL WARREN'S CORPS AT JERICHO FORD. IT WAS HERE THAT THE FEDERAL SOLDIERS MET WITH NO OPPOSITION. IN THE PICTURE AT THE TOP OF THE PAGE, WE SEE JERICHO MILL ON THE NORTH BANK. AN AMMUNITION TRAIN IS WINDING DOWN THE ROAD TO THE CROSSING. THE PICTURE, SHOWN AT THE BOTTOM (Right), SHOWS THE KIND OF COUNTRY THAT LAY BEYOND THE BRIDGE

About this time Lee was reinforced by fifteen thousand men,—a number not quite half what he had lost in the battles of the weeks before. Lee was able to bring this additional body of men to bear against Grant's attack due to the failure of the Federal troops at Yorktown to carry out commands. At the start of the campaign, General Butler, in charge of the Federal forces at Yorktown, was ordered to move towards Richmond and, at least, seize Petersburg. He moved westward early in May, but General Beauregard, who commanded the Southern troops, completely outwitted him and, on the 16th, Butler found himself, in his own words "bottled up" at Bermuda Hundreds, a peninsula, twenty miles south of Richmond, formed by a sharp bend of the James River.

This was a great disappointment to Grant for it disrupted his whole campaign and permitted the reinforcing of Lee's Army. Instead of trying to get Butler out of the trap into which he had fallen, Grant told him to dig his way out and this is, literally, what Butler tried to do. Early in August, he set to work, with all hands, to dig a canal at Dutch Gap to save a circuit of six miles in the bend of the James and thus avoid the batteries and torpedoes and obstructions which the Confederates had skilfully placed in controlling positions along the channel of the river.

133

THE USELESS CANAL BY MEANS OF WHICH GENERAL BUTLER HOPES TO ESCAPE

It took General Butler all the rest of the year, 1864, to cut through the high banks that hemmed him in. Meanwhile, of course, his men were exposed to the fire of Confederate batteries. This feat of the General's was one of the humorous incidents of the war and it is said that Grant and his fellow Generals followed the operations with a glint of humor in their serious eyes. To bring Butler's folly to a proper climax, he made an effort, just before the war closed, to blow up the dam at the mouth of the canal. The result was unsuccessful.

CITY POINT . . . AT THE JUNCTION OF THE JAMES AND THE APPOMATTOX RIVERS

Here are two views of the busiest place in Dixie. From June 1864 until April 1865, this place was a point of entry and departure for more vessels than any other city in the South, including even New Orleans in times of peace. Supplies landed here, kept an army of one hundred, twenty thousand men well fed and well supplied with all the munitions of war. It was meals and money more than arms and men that captured Richmond, according to the testimony of impartial historians.

AT THIS POINT ON THE NORTH ANNA RIVER, GRANT LEFT A STRONG DETACHMENT AS A REAR GUARD. THE PLACE IS JERICHO MILLS AND THE DATE, THE LAST OF MAY

———————————

BEHIND SUCH ENTRENCHMENTS AS THESE THE CONFEDERATES WAITED FOR THE ATTACK

BY SUCH MASSES OF CAVALRY, GRANT SCREENED HIS REAL PURPOSE TO CHANGE HIS BASE TO THE PAMUNKEY RIVER

GRANT'S SOLDIERS FORAGING ON THE WAY TO COLD HARBOR. THESE MEN WERE PHOTOGRAPHED WHILE DIGGING POTATOES

137

TEN THOUSAND MEN FELL IN THIS SPOT

WHERE THE FEDERAL CAMP STOOD AFTER
THE BATTLE OF COLD HARBOR

By a skilful recall of his divided forces, Grant was able to escape from the trap Lee had laid for him. He was aided in his escape by the fact that Lee, hoping for further help from the South, delayed an attack on a grand scale. Once more, Grant, finding the Confederate positions too strong to take by storm, moved to the left in a great flanking movement which began on the 26th of May. On the 25th Sheridan and his Cavalry had rejoined the army, after a most successful raid that had carried them to the first line of defenses around Richmond, itself.

At the close of May, Grant reached the banks of the Chickahominy River, very near the spot where the battle of Cold Harbor had been fought two years before. Lee, as usual, was already on the spot, waiting for his opponent,—behind heavily constructed positions. This is what General Grant, himself, said about the battle that took place shortly after the arrival of the troops:

"Cold Harbor is, I think, the only battle I ever fought that I would not fight over again under the circumstances. I have always regretted that the last assault at Cold Harbor was ever made."—"Memoirs."

Grant made up his mind to attack the Confederate entrenchments. It was his hope that by defeating them as they stood, through the cavalry of General Sherman, he could cut off their retreat and thus bring the war to a close. Preliminary skirmishing began on the 31st of May.

THIS IS THE CRUDE BREASTWORK THROWN UP BY THE CONFEDERATE SOLDIERS AT
THE END OF THE BATTLE LINE. EVERY LULL IN THE FIGHTING WAS SEIZED
BY BOTH SIDES TO STRENGTHEN DEFENCES

BURNETT'S HOUSE NEAR COLD HARBOR: BEFORE THIS HOUSE POSED THE VERY MEN,
WHO, A FEW HOURS BEFORE, IN THE SAME SPOT, HAD REPELLED
A TERRIFIC CONFEDERATE ATTACK

On the 3d of June the real battle began. In the gray dawn of a rainy morning
the Federal troops moved forward to the attack. They were met with a withering
fire and forced to fall back. The battle lasted hardly more than an hour but seven
thousand Northern soldiers fell on the field. The Confederates, behind their entrenchments, did not lose as many as that. Once again, the veteran Lee had held
his own against the mightiest force the North could send against him. Grant had
much to think about. His object was to capture Richmond, but Lee lay across his
path. He finally decided, after several days of delay, to begin his flanking movement once more and approach the Capital of the Confederacy from the east and
south. He began extending his lines to the left. Lee matched every move he made.
The lines were often so close together that sharpshooters could pick off the men as
they worked in the trenches. On the 7th of June there was a brief truce during
which each side buried its dead.

The movement towards the James River began in earnest on the 12th of June
when Warren's corps crossed the Chickahominy by the long bridge shown in the
picture below.

139

GRANT'S PREPARATIONS FOR THE SIEGE OF PETERSBURG WERE VERY THOROUGH. ABOVE, WE SEE MEN IN THE ACT OF STRINGING WIRES FOR THE TELEGRAPH SYSTEM, THAT HE INSTALLED

CHAPTER THIRTEEN

The Siege of Petersburg

General Lee at first thought that it was Grant's purpose to move on Richmond along the north bank of the James River. He, therefore, also crossed the Chickahominy and fell back to strong entrenchments that he had prepared months before not far from Richmond. His army, at that time, numbered about seventy thousand men. Lee had reason to believe that with this force he could hold Richmond against any assault. It was necessary, however, that his men be well-fed and cared for in every military way. Richmond was a well-fortified city. The entrenchments consisted of low mounds with trenches behind them in which men could be fairly safe from rifle fire. At various important points strong forts had been built.

Below Richmond, however, was another city into which several railroads poured a constant stream of traffic destined for the Capital itself. The Richmond Railroad entered from the north. The City Point Railroad entered from the northeast. The Norfolk Railroad entered from the southeast, the Weldon Railroad, from the south and the Southside Railroad, from the west. These railroads have been mentioned by name to show how important a center *Petersburg* was at the time and how reasonable it was that Grant should besiege *it*, instead of wasting time, men and effort trying to take the final objective, Richmond, itself.

(*Narrative is continued on page* 144)

THE PICTURES ON THIS PAGE GIVE US A SPLENDID IDEA OF HOW THE CROSSING OF THE JAMES RIVER WAS SUCCESSFULLY ACCOMPLISHED. IN THE RIGHT, LOWER, PICTURE, WE SEE A SECTION OF A PONTOON BRIDGE BEING SET IN PLACE

CHARLES CITY COURT HOUSE ON THE JAMES RIVER. NEAR THIS SPOT THE JAMES WAS CROSSED BY GRANT'S TROOPS. THIS PICTURE WAS TAKEN ON JUNE 14TH, 1864

Until the arrival of Grant, no one seemed to appreciate the importance of Petersburg and recognize it as the key to Richmond. Because of this fact it was practically without fortifications. In fact what fortifications it had were so feeble that they had been ridden over by Federal Cavalry early in May.

When Grant reached the scene shown above, he sighed with relief. His flanking movement around Lee's right had been a very dangerous one. At times, over fifty miles had separated him from General Butler, who was trapped at Bermuda Hundreds. It was Grant's task not only to prevent the Southern army from attacking while the movement of troops and supplies went on, but to hold Lee so firmly that he could not swing south, and destroy Butler's army before it could be given aid.

Lee had the shorter roads over which to travel, but said Grant, "the move had to be made and I relied on Lee's not seeing my danger as I saw it."

When the troops had safely crossed the James River, Grant went up to Bermuda Hundreds to see General Butler and direct the movement against Petersburg. From this moment the cause of the Confederacy rapidly declined.

On the evening of June 16th, Grant made an attack on Petersburg in force. The Confederates bitterly contested every inch of the ground. For a moment it seemed as though Petersburg would be taken. The first defences were stormed. At that instant, General Beauregard rallied his forces and, with the assistance of troops summoned from before Bermuda Hundreds, held back the Northern soldiers until darkness fell.

Lee, now fully aware of the importance of Petersburg, hurried down from Richmond with reinforcements. Another battle followed. Ten thousand men had fallen, when Grant decided that the attempt to carry the place by storm was too costly. On the 19th of June, he settled down for a long siege.

Grant was very thorough in his preparations for the struggle. In the scene above, we have a view of the telegrapher's tent. The batteries were located in the wagon and the whole outfit was designed for swift movement from place to place. Grant counted on attempts by the Southern forces to raid his equipment and obtain supplies by swift counter strokes. With the electric telegraph constantly keeping his headquarters informed of every movement, he was in a position to head off such efforts instantly.

Within two days, the Federal soldiers had thrown up strong entrenchments that paralleled those of the defenders. It now became the task of Grant to cut the railroads that still remained open. At a cost of over five thousand men the Weldon and Danville roadbeds were destroyed and at once the spectre of famine began to haunt the minds of the Confederate leaders. In commenting on this phase of his work, Grant said, "the damage suffered by the enemy in this expedition more than compensated for all the losses we sustained." Wheat became scarce in Petersburg and the value of Confederate money dropped sharply.

In spite of the dangerous position Lee was now in, he continued to put up a powerful front. His army was still the sturdy force that had fought Grant in the Wilderness, foiled him at Spottsylvania, checked him on the North Anna River and defeated him on the Chickahominy. The picture was different on the Federal side. Grant had lost nearly half of his best officers and trained men. Many of the new recruits were poor soldiers, due to hasty training.

A HOUSE NEAR WASHINGTON STRUCK BY ONE OF EARLY'S SHELLS

Grant was not slow to realize that, under such circumstances, unless he used great caution, the tables might be turned in an hour and his whole force driven back to its bases on the coast. The instant Grant slackened his efforts to seize Petersburg by force, Lee sent his able General Early northward for another attack on Washington. With remarkable speed the Confederate forces swept into Maryland and on the 10th of July came within six miles of the Capital.

Grant hurried reinforcements northward and these arrived just in time to save Washington from capture. Early retreated across the Potomac, but was so feebly pursued that he turned, drove once more across the river, and captured Chambersburg, Pennsylvania. He levied a ransom of two hundred thousand dollars in gold against the citizens. When it was not paid, he set fire to the houses and escaped.

THE RUINS OF CHAMBERSBURG, PENNSYLVANIA

GRANT MADE GOOD USE OF BALLOONS IN KEEPING HIMSELF INFORMED OF MOVEMENTS
BEYOND THE LINES. IN THE PICTURE SHOWN ABOVE, THE OBSERVER
IN THE BALLOON CAR IS ACTUALLY WATCHING THE ENEMY

145

THESE ARE THE MEN WHO WERE GIVEN THE TASK OF RUSHING INTO THE CONFEDERATE LINES THE INSTANT THE MINE EXPLODED

Towards the end of July, Grant felt that he had the situation well in hand and the active siege of Petersburg once more was undertaken. A division of Butler's Army had taken up positions ten miles below Richmond. Grant hoped that the presence of this strong force would compel Lee to withdraw some of his troops from Petersburg. In that case, he planned an immediate assault. Meanwhile, he began the building of a mine under the outer fortifications of the doomed town. This mine was five hundred and twenty feet long and was charged with eight thousand pounds of powder. It exploded on the afternoon of July 30th. A force of fifty thousand men rushed forward and plunged into the immense crater left by the explosion. They were unable to climb out again and the Confederates, standing on the rim, mowed down eight thousand men. Grant blamed himself bitterly for this terrible catastrophe.

146

THE HOLE DUG BY EIGHT THOUSAND POUNDS OF POWDER

IN A DESPERATE EFFORT TO PREVENT THE EXPLOSION UNDER THEIR FORT, THE
CONFEDERATES DUG A MINE OF THEIR OWN. THIS IS THE OPENING
THROUGH WHICH THEY ENTERED IT

SUCH DEFENCES AS THOSE SHOWN ON THIS PAGE CONVINCED GRANT THAT PETERSBURG COULD NOT BE TAKEN BY ASSAULT, AND FOR FIVE WEEKS HE RESTED ON HIS ARMS

The two armies seemed, at this time, to be dead-locked. Meanwhile, as shall be seen in Book Two, important operations, going on elsewhere, were having a vital effect upon the outcome of the struggle. Sheridan had begun the destruction of the Shenandoah Valley. While this struggle was going on, the Army of the Potomac prepared to go into winter quarters before Petersburg. While the forces of the North lived *well*, those of the South were being gradually weakened by starvation.

THESE STRANGE BASKETS WERE MADE OF WILLOW WANDS AND TWIGS CLOSELY WOVEN INTO A CIRCULAR CONTAINER INTO WHICH SAND AND EARTH COULD BE POURED. THEY WERE VERY EFFECTIVE IN STOPPING RIFLE BULLETS

AN ENGINE BEING UNLOADED FROM A TRANSPORT. IT IS TO BE USED IN THE SIEGE OF PETERSBURG TO DRAW SUCH GUN CARRIAGES AS THAT SHOWN BELOW INTO FIRING POSITIONS

While the armies ceased from active fighting, except for the constant sniping of sharpshooters, Grant was not idle. In every possible way he strengthened his own defences and made preparations for the renewal of the fight early in the spring. The pictures on this page show the nature of some of these preparations. Behind Grant was the wealth and industry of a mighty nation grimly determined now to undergo any sacrifice for victory. On the 15th of January 1865, Fort Fisher, which commanded the Port of Wilmington, was captured by the Federal Army. This was a terrible blow for Lee, since it shut off one of the most important avenues through which he received supplies.

ON THIS PAGE AND THE ONE OPPOSITE, TWO PICTURES OF GREAT HISTORICAL
IMPORTANCE ARE SHOWN. THESE GUNS ARE BEING FIRED DURING
THE SIEGE OF PETERSBURG

As spring approached, Lee was wise enough to see that the cause of the Confederacy was doomed. He had watched with anxious eye the preparation that Grant was slowly making. Caught in a gigantic web, he could do little while his methodical opponent, strand by strand, wound around him and his army bands of steel which rapidly reached such strength that no power at Lee's command could burst them asunder. It was evident that, before long, both Richmond and Petersburg would have to be abandoned. Lee had hoped that he could still offer resistance in the mountainous regions of Virginia and North Carolina. In order to reach this region, he began to plan some way of getting his army out of Richmond. Grant foresaw all this and was constantly on his guard against any attempt in force.

On the 29th of March, 1865, Grant began a movement against the Confederate right. Lee, to counter this, struck at the Federal center. He was thrown back with heavy loss. On April 1st, Sheridan won a decisive victory over Lee's forces at Five Forks, capturing more than five thousand men.

In this attempt Lee had stripped the defences of Petersburg of many thousands of defenders. Grant knew this and at once ordered an attack. It was against strong positions like that shown below that this attack was made. The outer works were carried with a heavy loss of men.

AS THE BATTLE ROARED . . . THESE MEN ARE PICKING OFF ADVANCING SOLDIERS

It was Sunday, and Jefferson Davis was at church in Richmond. When Lee saw the Federal soldiers swarm over the tops of the parapets that protected his outer lines, his first thought was for the safety of his leader. He went at once to his tent and sent a telegraph message in which he told Davis of what had happened and expressed his belief that Petersburg would have to be abandoned at once. Davis received the news calmly. He had foreseen its coming for many days. He at once gave orders to abandon Richmond. In order to give the troops in the Capital time to retreat, Lee clung to the defences of Petersburg. At night fall he still held some of the trenches. Grant rested, for he thought another day of hard fighting was ahead.

THE GUNS WERE IN ACTION AS THIS PICTURE WAS TAKEN. NOTE THE TENSE ATTITUDES OF THE GUNNERS AS THEY WATCH THEIR SHELLS EXPLODE

152

FIVE DIFFERENT VIEWS OF THE ENTRENCHMENTS THAT FIGURED IN THE BATTLE BEFORE PETERSBURG

UNDER SUCH CONDITIONS AS THESE SOLDIERS FOUGHT AND DIED BY THOUSANDS

154

THESE MEN WERE CAUGHT BY THE CAMERA AS THEY CHEERED THEIR COMRADES. THE SCENE WAS TAKEN AT THE MOMENT WHEN THE FEDERAL SOLDIERS, FOR THE FIRST TIME, STORMED AND CAPTURED THE OUTER DEFENCES OF PETERSBURG

At two o'clock, on Monday morning, the Confederate pickets were still on duty. Grant slept little that night. Tomorrow's dawn would tell a grim tale. He had little doubt of victory but he knew that he still had Lee to contend with and while that General remained in command there was always the chance of some unforeseen development. However, there was little cause for worry. At three o'clock Lee had completed the evacuation of Petersburg. His troops were all across the Appomattox River, the only bridge was in flames and the warehouses along the river's edge were being destroyed. Explosion after explosion told Grant the news of his enemy's retreat.

THE STORM HAS PASSED . . . A SCENE OF DEVASTATION REMAINS TO TELL THE STORY OF THE LAST FIGHT FOR A CAUSE IN WHICH MILLIONS OF AMERICANS FIRMLY BELIEVED

FOR THESE DEAD ALL WAR IS PAST FOREVER

156

In Richmond, the night was one of terror and sudden death. No sooner had Jefferson Davis left the city than mobs of looters swarmed through the streets breaking into houses and robbing the inhabitants. To make matters worse, General Ewell set fire to the bridges and warehouses. The conflagration spread rapidly and, in a few hours, over one third of Richmond was in flames. The pictures on this page tell a terrible story of the ruin that resulted,—not from Federal shells but from the torches of Southerners, themselves.

A FEDERAL WAGON TRAIN MOVES OUT OF PETERSBURG TO FEED THE ARMY THAT IS PURSUING THE FLEEING SOUTHERN SOLDIERS

At half past four that afternoon the Federal flag was raised above Petersburg. Arrangements were made at once to take up the pursuit of the retreating forces. Grant, unlike McClellan, lost no opportunity to harrass his foe. Lee's purpose was to retreat to Danville, where he hoped to unite his shattered forces with those of General Johnston. His men were widely scattered and must be brought together under one command if they were to serve, effectively, the cause of the Confederacy. At Burkesville two railroads joined. He had hopes of reaching that spot and destroying the tracks so as to impede pursuit. He was aided in this plan by spring freshets that slowed down the march of troops whenever a small stream was to be crossed.

Lee had marched out of Petersburg with only a single day's rations for his men. Trains loaded with supplies were to meet him at Amelia Court House, half way between Richmond and Burkesville.

ONE OF THE FLOODED STREAMS THAT OFFERED LEE A CHANCE TO ESCAPE

BEHIND GRANT A STEADY STREAM OF SUPPLIES FLOWED FROM THE
JAMES RIVER TO THE FRONT

On reaching Amelia Court House, Lee was astonished to learn that his commands had been misunderstood and the trains had gone right on with the result that all of their precious foodstuffs had fallen into the hands of Federal raiders. This was, indeed, a terrible blow. The men were hungry and weak with fatigue. Lee was compelled to pause long enough to send out foraging squads. The delay was fatal to all his plans. The Federal troops were slowly overtaking his rear. Desperate rear guard battles took place. Thousands died in these useless conflicts. The end was drawing near.

A PLACE OF BITTER DISAPPOINTMENT FOR LEE AND HIS FAMISHED ARMY

159

THE McLEAN HOUSE IN APPOMATTOX, VIRGINIA. IT WAS IN THIS HOUSE THAT LEE AWAITED THE ARRIVAL OF GENERAL GRANT

On the 7th of April, 1865, Grant wrote to Lee proposing the surrender of his army. Grant's terms were generous and Lee, convinced that any further fighting was a sheer waste of precious blood, consented. On the 9th, the two Generals met at Appomattox. Under the terms of that document the soldiers of the South were allowed to return to their homes without punishment of any kind.

APPOMATOX COURT HOUSE WHERE THE TWO GENERALS SIGNED THE FINAL TERMS OF SURRENDER

160